Journey to a High-Achieving School

Eliminate Destructive Excuses

Fred J. Abbate, Ken Biddle, and
Joseph M. Tomaselli

ROWMAN & LITTLEFIELD EDUCATION
A division of
ROWMAN & LITTLEFIELD PUBLISHERS, INC.
Lanham • New York • Toronto • Plymouth, UK

Published by Rowman & Littlefield Education
A division of Rowman & Littlefield Publishers, Inc.
A wholly owned subsidiary of The Rowman & Littlefield Publishing Group, Inc.
4501 Forbes Boulevard, Suite 200, Lanham, Maryland 20706
www.rowman.com

10 Thornbury Road, Plymouth PL6 7PP, United Kingdom

Copyright © 2013 by Fred J. Abbate, Ken Biddle, and Joseph M. Tomaselli

All rights reserved. No part of this book may be reproduced in any form or by any electronic or mechanical means, including information storage and retrieval systems, without written permission from the publisher, except by a reviewer who may quote passages in a review.

British Library Cataloguing in Publication Information Available

Library of Congress Cataloging-in-Publication Data

Abbate, Fred, 1939–
Journey to a high-achieving school : eliminate destructive excuses / Fred J. Abbate, Ken Biddle, and Joseph M. Tomaselli.
pages cm.
Includes bibliographical references.
ISBN 978-1-4758-0044-9 (cloth : alk. paper)—ISBN 978-1-4758-0045-6 (pbk. : alk. paper)—ISBN 978-1-4758-0046-3 (electronic) 1. School improvement programs—United States. 2. Educational change—United States. 3. Educational leadership—United States. I. Title.
LB2822.82.A25 2013
371.2'07—dc23
2013000267

Contents

Preface		v
1	Why Another Book about Education?	1
2	The Excuse-Riddled Mindset	5
3	Defeating the Excuses, Part 1	15
4	Defeating the Excuses, Part 2	33
5	Can These Things Work in Any School? Even Mine? You're Kidding!	53
6	Every Journey Has a Few Potholes: Here's Some Help in How to Handle Them	99
Appendix A: The Lessons of Authentic Leadership		113
Appendix B: An Authentic Leader's Self-Assessment		115
Appendix C: *IDEAS* Project Report Template		119
Appendix D: Additional Resources		121
Glossary		123
About the Authors		125

Preface

The major ideas on which this book is based are the essential concepts used in the Performance Excellence Group's *Academy for Education Leaders*, the program that the authors have been conducting for several years in New Jersey for school superintendents, principals, and other members of their key educational teams. The program itself requires eight full-day sessions of intense work over as many months, and those enrolled concentrate on specific issues in order to make measurable progress toward higher achievement in their schools.

We came to believe in time that the important quality tools at the heart of the Academy should be shared with a wider audience of educators to help them begin a more analytical reexamination of their major policies and processes. For a written version of the Academy concepts, however, an alternative approach had to be developed, since we would not be able to engage readers in the face-to-face and extended interaction we have with our program participants. So we concluded that we could make the methods of the Academy accessible to first-timers by positioning them as rebuttals to excuses offered for educational underachievement.

METHODOLOGY

The excuses we selected are the rationalizations that we have heard more than once to justify avoiding the tough work it takes to change a school or school district for the better. We begin by listing these excuses as forthrightly as we can, then setting a climate within which they can be addressed. After speaking to them provisionally, we specifically apply the system's thinking and leadership tools to them, and close with a kind of road map for negotiating through problems that might get in the way of success. Our hope is that by the final chapter educational professionals will have come to appreciate the more complete and connected picture of our Academy's methodology and see it as more than a remedy for separate attempts to explain away a school's deficiencies.

Readers will likely detect a slightly whimsical strain in the tone we take as we describe and handle the excuses, but our aim is to suggest the ambiance we try to generate in our actual Academy sessions. We are doing serious work, of course, and no one should have any doubt about its importance. Nevertheless, it is work that is done in an atmosphere of collegiality and even humor; inspired, we hope, by the model of good teaching anywhere. We are quite aware of and appreciate some of the very valuable studies that address educational improvement—we will point a few out in the pages that follow—but we wanted our book to be as approachable as we could make it, to speak more personally to readers rather than make academic speeches to them.

We are confident that the strategies and methods we having been using in the Academy and in related consulting work with schools are both unique and, with commitment and practice, can lead to highly effective outcomes. First, what we believe is distinctive about our approach is the merging of systems thinking and leadership skill into a unified way of dealing with problems, decisions, planning, action, and accountability. What we call "authentic leadership" practices are not grafted on as shaky afterthoughts to process thinking.

High-performing organizations, whether they be schools, hospitals, or auto dealerships have leaders who understand that excellence requires data-driven policies. These are leaders who embody the essence of the enterprise's mission, vision, values, and goals in all that they say and do. Every single step in the methodology we use—a process we call *IDEAS*—requires an investment in leadership that makes a positive difference to performance excellence.

Secondly, and regarding the effectiveness of the methods, the dozens of educational leaders who have been through our Academy and with whom we have consulted stand as our clearest criterion of success. They consistently and enthusiastically tell us about the measurable gains they have made in solving major problems in their schools and in establishing a culture of higher performance.

And just as importantly, many of the superintendents who have completed the Academy seminars enroll the key team members who report to them in successive sessions of the program. We have included some examples throughout the book of the progress we want every education leader to achieve, and many of the examples we underscore to illustrate the critical principles are the result of actual cases we have dealt with in other organizations—schools, nonprofits, and businesses.

READERSHIP

While the administrative leadership is the principal audience for the systems thinking and leadership concepts we develop in the following chapters, it would be a mistake to assume that others involved in the teaching and learning enterprise will not gain from working with them. A point we will keep reminding readers of throughout the book—one might even say we will keep harping on—is that the tools for improvement work only in collaboration with all who have responsibility for insuring an excellent educational outcome.

These concepts have value for all decision makers—superintendents, principals, supervisors, school-board members, teachers, and even students. When these methods become second nature to the entire school system and part of the very fiber of how they do business, there is almost no stopping their progress toward significantly higher achievement.

ORGANIZATION

After a brief first-chapter discussion of the particular approach we will be taking in the pages ahead, chapter 2 lays out some of the details of the excuse-riddled mindset, namely, the list of major excuses we have either encountered in our work with administrators, teachers, school-board members, and other educational players, or know about them from a variety of research work and other kinds of studies.

We have tried in this chapter to argue as strong a case as we can for these excuses, so that readers will appreciate their plausibility and how they might have ensnared even the most conscientious spirits of some educational decision makers. It is essential to note that educators who proffer some of these justifications for failure truly believe they are not simply cop outs for avoiding hard work, but factually based on realities over which they have no real hope of control.

In our third chapter we argue that defeating the excuses for failure has to begin by adopting an entirely new outlook on addressing educators' frustrations—in effect, with an entirely different fresh start to a whole new attitude and philosophy. To us that philosophy begins with the indispensable role that authentic leadership must play in this transformation. It involves acting to strive for performance excellence in a focused, disciplined, and consciously systematic way. Our viewpoint embraces clear and steadfast attention to the mission, vision, values, and goals of any organization, and we will address what these concepts really mean and what they unambiguously imply about building a culture of genuine success.

Chapter 4 begins to introduce the essential tools for dealing with the issues that actually lie behind the litany of excuses for low achievement. The representative justifications for failure we gave some credence to in chapter 2 are now examined more specifically to show that total loss of control is not part of their (or our) DNA. There are some general ways and realistic approaches that can be used to make measurable progress in bringing these tough issues under control. The aim here is not to totally eliminate the excuses, but to begin to show that elimination is not only possible but can be workable, since other organizations and school districts have addressed these problems successfully by rethinking their approach.

Once we have this broader handle on how to start moving in the right direction, we introduce and discuss the more detailed concepts and powerful tools of systems thinking in our fifth chapter. We believe that the most successful eradication of the excuses should take place in two phases. Since the generalized stage-setting approaches discussed in chapter 4 might still appear too abstract for some readers, we draw an in-depth picture of the critical steps on the journey to high achievement and illustrate the essential tools needed to successfully start making headway.

This double-barreled approach to introducing the concepts, by the way, is exactly how we deploy it in our Academy, and we have tried to exemplify the use of the tools by describing some cases we have actually worked with. We could quite reasonably have called this chapter "Defeating the Excuses Again," but decided to stress the idea that these very powerful tools can work effectively in just about any educational environment.

Leadership again plays a key role in this discussion of system thinking—it always will in the pursuit of excellence. Here we place emphasis on techniques for priority setting, finding the root causes of major problems, decision making based on true consensus and relevant data, and the effective ways to deploy improvement plans, assign responsibilities, and monitor progress. Throughout the chapter, we will keep trying to demonstrate, by examples based on our own work with educational leaders, the concrete approaches that can be taken and that we know can make a critical difference.

We understand that the journey to achieving a culture of excellence and high achievement is not a trouble-free trip, and our chapter 6 might, therefore, be called the "reality check" part of our book. There are potholes, obstacles, barriers, and other problems on any trip, of course. So here we try to underscore the vital need to think longer-range, celebrate the small ground gains that are being made, and avoid the frustration that can often accompany disappointing results on the first few tries. Of course, this is easier said than done, since the old pressures from the community, regulators, special-agenda holders, and others who have a stake in things staying exactly the way they are will not suddenly disappear.

MOVING FORWARD

Each chapter concludes with specific ideas for further consideration, and we hope these suggestions and exercises will be discussed with the readers' colleagues and explored in a truly collaborative way. The real power of genuine systems thinking and authentic leadership lies in its not becoming thought of as the special prerogatives of the few. They must be shared as widely as possible. Good ideas in any department of life are not usually the result of thinking in isolation from others, especially from those who have a major stake in and a duty for seeking success. One reason we know why our Academy works so well is that our leader-participants are not passive individualists, but work with, constantly help, and regularly learn from each other.

As instructors, we, too, have learned a great deal from our participants. We will without doubt keep learning from them and look forward to the value they will keep offering to us. We gratefully acknowledge their help and thank them for the enthusiasm and professional dedication they continue to display in the extremely important work that they do.

Fred J. Abbate
Ken Biddle
Joseph M. Tomaselli

ONE
Why Another Book about Education?

He who excuses himself accuses himself. —French proverb

Imagine that you receive the following letter a few weeks before your son or daughter starts the new school year:

Dear Mr. and Mrs. Parent:
We are certainly looking forward to having your child with us at the start of another school year and will do our very best to make sure that it will be a productive experience.
I need to warn you, however, not to have high expectations for your child, since there are a whole range of things that are going to make educational quality very doubtful for our students—things over which we have absolutely no control and which will make the pursuit of progress in our schools extremely difficult. I won't try to bore you with the details right now, but there simply isn't much we can do about these things.
The teachers union is digging in its heels against any meaningful changes we have been trying to make, and prospects for compromise are very slim. A maze of new federal and state regulations are becoming more and more burdensome and make innovative approaches in our school just about impossible. And to top it off, as I'm sure you know, this community doesn't seem the least bit interested in supporting education in any serious way, has no idea what we are trying to accomplish, and can't be counted upon to provide help, financial or otherwise, for our mission.
We have tried to deal with these issues, but there is very little hope that anything can be done about them, short of some miracle. We simply have to face the facts and have to be realistic. Nevertheless, we will keep trying to give every

child our best effort. I wanted to be sure, however, that you were prepared for severe disappointment as early as possible and that you understood the insurmountable difficulties that we are facing.

Very truly yours,
  Dr. J. R. Average, District Superintendent

All right, it is certainly hard to actually imagine an educational leader sending such a letter to school parents, in effect a public confession that failure is the only true option for the school system. And yet—privately, of course—are there not times at many levels of the educational enterprise when it appears that disappointment is not only expected but, perhaps, inevitable—that the problems standing in the way of significant educational improvement and higher quality have grown interminable and even insuperable?

The school board is too political and not interested in giving our teachers any real support, one might hear. The students don't see any value to education, probably because of the signals that their peers, their parents, and the mindless culture keep sending them. The faculty is burned out and more focused on pension and other benefits than on effective teaching and learning. The list could go on and on, a list of problems whose causes we seem unable to get a handle on, let alone solve, a list that functions for us as our special catalogue of excuses.

Let's think a little more about excuses. What does using them actually imply? Speaking generally, to offer an excuse is to give a reason why (a) something that needed to be done was not done or (b) something was done that should not have been done. Excuses, of course, can be perfectly legitimate. If I promised to drive a friend to an important appointment and I fail to show up, I might offer as good excuses that my car would not start, or it was damaged by vandals, stolen, and so on. But excuses can also be unjustified as well. I forgot my promise, I overslept, I had the wrong day on my calendar.

When the thing that has to be accomplished is very important, the excuse for not doing it or doing it badly *has to be clearly and compellingly justified*—especially if the excuse is part of a chronic litany of rationalizations. The surgeon who offers constant excuses for botched operations would hardly inspire patient confidence. Nor would the attorney who recited one excuse after another for losing case after case.

Leading a life of excuses—constantly and consistently throwing up one's hands and claiming that the important job one has been charged with cannot be done or cannot be done well because of forces beyond anyone's control—is leading *the life of a victim*. It is the life of the persistently and haplessly injured party.

- Victims do not act; they are the people who are *acted upon* by something or someone. The very definition of the word entails this. We might feel sorry for them, but we have no real expectations of them from the viewpoint of taking charge of their own predicament.
- Victims are, therefore, *not risk takers*; they tend to look at the world as a place overflowing with disappointments, traps, or problems, not opportunities. Truly innovative approaches to those problems are generally out of the question for them.
- Victims incline toward finding someone or something to *blame* for their situation, not toward trying to find the *real cause* of the problem they are having or the barriers they claim they simply cannot overcome.

Here's a silly question: How important is the education of our children? Would anyone in his or her right mind think it is unimportant? Can we even conceive of a truly significant future for our society without an excellent education for those who will inherit that future?

And yet, what kind of rational sense does it make to keep claiming excuses for not getting the job done successfully? What we would never for a moment tolerate as a chronicle of offered excuses for severe and unvarying failure by a doctor, a lawyer, or an automotive mechanic have somehow gotten into our consciousness as perfectly acceptable—even perfectly legitimate—when it comes to educational quality. The damage done by the unfortunate schools and school systems that settle for such victimhood, for this "inevitable" mediocrity and chronic failure is certainly as destructive to the human condition as almost anything we can think of.

Now, no one would ever deny that the work of education is an exceptionally challenging occupation and a vocation that seems to get more and more demanding with each passing year. If those challenges, however, are *classified as obstacles that cannot be surmounted*, the very possibility of dealing with them is doomed from square one. In some schools, we know from hard experience, this kind of surrender has resulted in a pervasive culture of pessimism, resignation, and even cynicism.

- Opportunities to improve are visualized as guaranteed invitations to fail before one has even gotten to the starting gate.
- New ideas are seen as just so many snares waiting in the underbrush to capture us.
- Success demonstrated in other schools or districts is quickly derided as gimmicky or not applicable to special issues of one's own case.

This is the appalling price paid for an educational world built around excuses, a culture whose principal perspective is blame, and for which genuine results-oriented action has become just about impossible .

The writers of this volume resolutely and passionately believe that *any* school or school district—no matter what state, city, or community it is in, no matter what kind of school it is, no matter what types of problems it is facing or has faced in the past, in short, *every school and every district*—can make significant and measurable progress toward becoming a high-achieving school, a special place where strong authentic leadership is in evidence, where students get an excellent education from motivated and effective teachers.

We believe this because we have seen this precise kind of progress made in many of the schools and with many of the school leaders we have worked with over several years, especially in the rigorous sessions we have conducted in our *Academy for Education Leaders*. Among the critical aims we have established for the Academy program are to help our participants to:

- Use the valuable tools of systems thinking to successfully address major issues and problems holding the school district back from higher-achievement for its students;
- Install outcome-based accountability into the very fabric of the school-district culture by authentic leadership;
- Build a sustainable, shared, and genuinely felt vision that serves as the framework against which major policies and programs are evaluated;
- Inspire a team-oriented and empowering approach to success at all levels and in all schools;
- Work more effectively with the district's board, parents, community, and governing bodies charged with oversight and regulation of education outcomes.

We believe that the key to high achievement requires the kind of leadership we have called *authentic*, leadership that settles for nothing less than the highest standards for every part of the organization. This means the uncompromising commitment to maximum accomplishment for every child, respect for the solid professionalism of teachers and staff, and the courage to make the tough changes necessary to push for a culture of excellence.

The journey to high achievement is not an easy one. There are no express trains for getting there, and more than a few people will be sometimes baffled and even battered on the trip. And perhaps there might be some problems that truly and really are outside of the control of even our best efforts. One thing, however, is certain: *unless we start the process of trying to eliminate the excuses we offer for lack of improvement, for failing to be the high-achieving organization we can and morally must be, this journey will never get started.*

TWO

The Excuse-Riddled Mindset

And oftentimes excusing of a fault doth make the fault worse by the excuse.
—Shakespeare

SOME PRELIMINARIES

Although there are probably endless excuses for educational failure, we're going to classify them into seven key groups to make them a bit easier to handle. (There seems something magically authoritative about that number. Seven veils? Seven Wonders of the World? Seven capital sins?)

Dozens of variations on these excuse categories are also possible—we'll note a few as we unpack them—but we think their essential character endures even when we tweak them into slightly mutated forms. We should also note that these categories are not airtight and that the description of any one of them will often engage points we'll make in describing others. After we explore a good helping of these excuses, our next two chapters will, we hope, begin to deploy some ways to address them.

One important point with respect to what we are doing here should be clearly emphasized before we begin. In exemplifying and addressing these excuses, *we are in no way suggesting that educators do not sincerely believe that they are based in reality and are truly justified*. Yes, educators, like any of us, can be guilty of self-deception at times, but our position is not that administrators and teachers are lying to themselves or shirking off their fundamental responsibilities.

Most of these professionals, we truly believe, really and sincerely hold that—despite their best efforts—many of these excuses are warranted, that the loss of control they are experiencing is based in case-hardened, pragmatic fact. Our aim is not to dole out blame to educators. We'll argue later than assigning blame seldom gets you anywhere when you're looking for why bad things happen. Rather, our intention is to get to the bottom of these beliefs, show that they are not only generally untrue, but dangerously so, because the longer they persist the more difficult it will be to do something meaningful about them.

All right, here are the seven categories.

- *"You just don't get our problem!"*
- *"Students just aren't interested in learning."*
- *"Our community doesn't support us; it's probably against us!"*
- *"Change is something that teachers by nature resist."*
- *"Tenure makes good teaching about as valuable as acne."*
- *"School leaders are really terrible models of excellence."*
- *"School-board politics will destroy every one of us anyway."*

EXCUSE NUMBER ONE: "YOU JUST DON'T GET OUR PROBLEM!"

This first excuse covers a pretty wide neighborhood. At its foundation seems to be the conviction that unless you have actually walked in the shoes of an educator, truly and concretely experienced what it is like to deliver the teaching and learning process, you cannot even begin to understand (a) how it is unlike anything else, (b) how astoundingly difficult it is, and (c) how solutions to problems that might work perfectly well in other departments of life simply don't have a snowball's chance in Hades of surviving here.

One common version of this excuse particularly targets any attempts we might make to use the systems of well-run business enterprises to help as models for educational improvement. "Education is *NOT* a business," one hears in some quarters, often with an implied sneer to strengthen its meaning. "The mission of our schools has nothing to do with profit-and-loss-statements or some quarterly bottom line to keep shareholders happy. We don't 'manage' people or manipulate markets—we are trying to educate citizens We care about them, we value them! And let's not forget that even very successful businesses can lose their way. Does anyone remember W. T. Grant, Braniff Airlines, Caldor, Tower Records?"

"What's more," the reply might continue, "we haven't got the freedom that the average entrepreneur or CEO has anyway, namely, the ability to experiment, to strike out in new and inventive directions. Even if the effective practices of businesses made sense for us, we live in a straightjacket that would bamboozle Houdini. We've got regulations coming out of our ears—rules from the Federal government, the state departments of education, the findings of 'special' commissions, the complex rules of union contracts, and heaven knows what else.

"And things get even worse when you realize that budgets are being cut to the bone and critical resources are drying up. Furthermore, as almost everyone knows by now, our performance as educators is being aggressively and unremittingly appraised by how our students do on test after test—standardized tests that are not of our own making and are of dubious value anyhow.

"These tests, by the way, catch us in a booby trap, too. Consider this: (a) if our students do well, we *get accused of teaching to the tests*—in other words, we're being complicit in the phony game of testing and not really educating students at all; (b) if our students do poorly on these tests, we are *again accused of failing to educate them*, since if they had been educated, they would have done better on the tests! If this isn't a lose/lose situation we've never seen one."

Not just practicing educators, but even theorists of educational policy sometimes put forth a version of this point. The writer Gordon Donaldson tells us that we "doom ourselves to failure"[1] if we think that schools respond to leaders the way businesses do. In short, the job that educators have to do is a very different ball game than what a business enterprise is about. Even the "ball game" metaphor can't be pushed too far, since Donaldson thinks that schools can't learn much from athletic squads or platoons either.

EXCUSE NUMBER TWO: "STUDENTS AREN'T INTERESTED IN LEARNING"

One of the key reasons that educational leaders often list to explain why things go so badly in our schools—a reason that also reinforces our first excuse—is that no matter how well the teachers teach and no matter how hard they work at trying to prepare their students, teachers are caught in a culture of low expectations where students just don't seem to want to learn. Of course, there are good students one can find anywhere, but the claim is that the *general trend* is toward mediocrity at best.

Administrators and teachers could argue, for example, that both the students and their parents "do not have high levels of aspiration, do not genuinely care about getting homework done, and are not interested in being challenged to intellectually grow." Parents and even some educators sometimes appear more interested in making sure that their children "have a meaningful educational experience," whether it entails actual learning or not.[2]

Chalking this up to some bigger social tidal waves of eroding ethical values, the superficiality of our digital age, poor diet, or the need for instant gratification, and whatever else might be defensible, but is not quite the point. "However we got to this juncture doesn't really matter," many educators would argue. "The reality is that we are dealing with a student and parent population that doesn't sincerely value the critical mission of our schools, namely, to turn out well-rounded people of sound judgment who can take a consequential place in society."

Educators might also point out that in districts where schools are clearly and abysmally failing, politicians often publicly blame the school leadership and the teachers for the failure, completely oblivious to the truth that no school can truly erase the effects that poverty, bad nutrition, and a nonsupportive home life clearly have on the readiness and willingness of students to actually learn.

"State lawmakers are particularly guilty of this ignorance, and, as if to avoid facing it, keep loading schools with new requirements," we also hear. "Some might be of some value, such as antibullying programs and nutritional curricula, but most have only slim and peripheral relationships to educational improvement. Moreover, they usually take time and energy from the mission. It is as if the school has become responsible not just for educating children but for raising them *in loco parentis*."

One effect of this dilution of the mission of schools, educators have noted, is that students have a difficult time understanding what they are to focus on, what exactly counts as a first-class education. "More and more," teachers and school leaders tell us, "we have to demonstrate a clear and certain connection between what is being taught and its relationship to a job or long-term career. Of course, we've known for a very long time that students need to see the relevance of learning to their lives. But classrooms are being subtly, but significantly, transformed into little more than training camps. The emphasis on critical thinking and judgment is slowly disappearing."

EXCUSE NUMBER THREE: "OUR COMMUNITY DOESN'T SUPPORT US; IT'S PROBABLY AGAINST US"

Many people probably know the old joke about the psychoanalyst's diagnosis of a patient who believes he is paranoid:

Patient: Go ahead, Doctor. I can take it.

Doctor: The good news is that you're not paranoid.

Patient: That's great! What's the bad news?

Doctor: Well, it turns out that they *really are* out to get you!

Educators at all levels these days might feel very much like that patient. Newspapers and television headlines proliferate with stories about local communities looking for someone to blame for their ever-increasing property taxes and other fees. Every year, in states where school budgets are submitted to the town or city's population, the proposals bite the dust, with the result that serious cuts have to be made in a range of important things for the school districts affected by the loss.

Some districts in several states have not voted affirmatively on a school budget in many years, believing that the spending plan is bloated with overblown and unnecessary accounts—in addition to the belief that how funds have already been spent in past years are packed with salary and benefits as well as other perks that bear little similarity to the way these are handled in noneducational enterprises.

Citizens are asking if all the money that has been spent in the name of improving education is worth it, given that no significant change in the quality of learning seems evident. One citizen at a school-board meeting in New Jersey was heard to say: "Stop throwing money at the problem. Or if you insist, then throw it at education, not the so-called educators."

Lately, as almost every news program has been covering extensively, educators and other public workers have been targeted in several states as the principal causes of the rising debts that states and municipalities are facing. Pensions are the prime suspect, although many other contentious issues bump up against this one, and as a result the public is asking if collective bargaining by public employees has gone too far and needs to be severely curtailed or even eliminated.

Education leaders are well aware of the tough spot this generally puts them in, an awareness that easily makes the move to genuine paranoia or clinical depression seem like a perfectly reasonable step. "Why bother to try to objectively present to our pubic the critical needs of the district and their true costs anymore," one educational leader in our Academy declaimed, "when the community we are serving thinks we're flimflam artists running some kind of Ponzi scheme, or that we are the primary reason why taxes are on the rise?"

"And it's not just about taxes," other leaders might add, "but the true consequences of the community's belief. If this is what our community members *really* think about the value we are bringing to their children and their futures, then trying to become a high-achieving school district for such a community sends us on a classic fool's errand. There is no trust in our integrity, no belief in our competence, and no backing and support when we need it."

EXCUSE NUMBER FOUR: "CHANGE IS SOMETHING THAT TEACHERS BY NATURE RESIST"

This excuse, one will easily note, is connected with Excuse Number Five, which we'll discuss below. It can, however, stand on its own in ways not linked with the tenure excuse.

Several administrators we have worked with over the years often assert that one of the most staggering obstacles to serious and systemic change in their schools resides right at home, namely, in the teaching staff itself. When asked why they believe this is true, they give some interesting answers. An administrator might grant, for instance, what most of us already know, namely, that all organizations tend to resist change to a greater or lesser extent. "The resistance, however, is much stronger in the teaching profession," the administrator might add, "because of *the very nature* of the teaching profession."

Teachers are inclined—and have been trained to be so inclined probably since the Middle Ages—to work within fairly inflexible structures of thinking and belief systems. Theirs is a world populated by preapproved curricula, measured and established standards that are decided well in advance, time-controlled interactions with students, days that are ordered in the same sequences. In short, it is a world that leaves little room, rhyme, or reason for innovation, a world where thinking "inside the box" is required as Standard Operating Procedure.

Of course, there are dozens of good, new ideas about how to improve teaching that emerge from some corner of the universe every year. Administrators point out, however, that "they usually get translated in ways that do not require any real change in how teachers go about their work. They become diluted, and whatever might have had real value often is squeezed out of them." It's one thing for a teacher to appreciate an innovative idea in the abstract; quite another to even recognize it once it has been filtered through a frame of mind that one has always been comfortable with for an entire professional career. As a result, the ideas lose whatever power they might have had to make for better outcomes.

The "union mentality" of the teaching profession doesn't help much either, many contend. Teachers, one hears administrators say, "tend to be suspicious of the administration—the 'management'—and chronically look for hidden agendas at work in so-called educational improvement schemes." Union-management relationships are defined by bargaining, and by its very nature bargaining is about getting the best possible deal from your opposite number. It's natural, then, to try to find the playing cards that are hidden up the sleeves of either party.

EXCUSE NUMBER FIVE: "TENURE MAKES GOOD TEACHING ABOUT AS VALUABLE AS ACNE"

This just might be the favored excuse that almost every education leader uses. Lately it's also the favored one of many political leaders as well and is used to justify why schools do not achieve at the highest levels.

Even if the excuse we've described above could be refuted or gotten around in some way, tenure, it will convincingly be pointed out by administrators and other education officials, "not only guarantees a job for life for the teacher, but does so in spite of the quality of job he or she does." Clearly, if bad teaching and good teaching are offered *the same guarantee,* the link between performance and accountability is wholly severed. And, of course, once that link is cut, the difference between good and bad teaching itself becomes next to meaningless.[3]

"Hold on!" some might reply. "Administrators might be exaggerating here. There is no actual 'guarantee,' since administrative codes in most states clearly define a procedure for dismissing incompetent or poor performing teachers, and several states as we speak are making tenure more difficult to obtain." However, administrators are quick to point out, in actual practice the procedures are so legally complex and cumbersome that it takes a great deal of time and bundles of money to build a credible case. In addition, the rules are generally weighted in favor of the teacher, they will add. This is why tenure is fast becoming the favorite target of some governors, mayors, and other officials. It is seen as the chief barricade standing in the way of teaching excellence.

This situation leads to what one might call "The Dead Wood Dilemma." Experience and longevity in a job are exactly the factors which are usually indicators of valued know-how and strength of judgment in most types of organizations. In education, however, they have instead become in and of themselves grounds for suspicion and mistrust.

EXCUSE NUMBER SIX: "SCHOOL LEADERS ARE REALLY TERRIBLE MODELS OF EXCELLENCE"

Teachers, as one might expect, have a rather different view of where some of the problems in education lie and, therefore, have their own special excuse for a school or district not becoming high achieving. They point to the fact that principals, superintendents, and other key education leaders do not (as the old saying has it) "walk the talk." Yes, these administrators are proud to unveil the latest and newest idea to come down from on high, but their own leadership style shows the emptiness and pretense of their solemn pronouncements.

"Administrators talk about the importance of collaboration and cooperation," teachers might contend, "but many of us have to work in an authoritarian environment where our opinions do not count any more than echoes in a wind tunnel. We are told that we are true professionals, but in fact we are treated as if we have the brains of a cantaloupe.

"We're told to take all the time we need to plan so we can make a genuine difference in our students' lives. We then see our leaders only respond to one invented crisis after another, and push us in the same hurried direction. The research has shown for decades that a school building and a school district have to reflect the values of their educational leaders. Without solid and constructive models for us and for our students all the preaching from administrators comes to nothing and progress becomes a cruel fraud."

EXCUSE NUMBER SEVEN: "SCHOOL-BOARD POLITICS WILL DESTROY EVERY ONE OF US ANYWAY"

This excuse for achieving only dismal mediocrity in a school system can be coupled with the excuse that blames the community, since, presumably, a school board in theory reflects the sentiments of the district's citizenry. Some boards, of course, are appointed and not elected, so doubt about whether they reflect anything more than some narrow political purpose is certainly reasonable.

Yet, even if board members are elected, an administrator or teacher may very well argue, the vote might manifest only the particular agenda of a minority of the community, perhaps a segment out to implement some small-minded ideological view. Local newspapers show this sort of thing constantly, as 'reform' candidates line up to "get educational costs under control" or demand changes in science or history textbooks, or get "immoral" literature out of the library.

As often as not, these agendas reflect some particular pique the elected or appointed board member has experienced firsthand, either in her or his own family or as a result of complaints by a neighbor. The anger or irritation then transforms itself into the need to pay someone back for incompetence or mismanagement, disguised as ideological fervor.

Boards of education, like boards of almost all types, are supposed to address and set broad policy, not manage the day-to-day affairs of the teachers, students, and administrators. Yet, education leaders keep informing us, this intrusion is happening all over the country. Much of the time and energy of the superintendent and his or her administrative team are spent trying to wrest control back to where it should be. Plainly, then, any genuine prospect of becoming a high-achieving district will be more fiction than fact in such an *Alice in Wonderland* setting.

A FEW REFLECTIONS

As we mentioned above, we'll be tackling these excuse categories in the next three chapters in a variety of increasing ways. But some final points about their general nature might be in order here. First, the list we've explored is not exhaustive, and has as many variations, combinations, and permutations as anything that might be imagined by a deranged geneticist. We believe, however, that the categories capture the main contours of an excuse culture, a culture that we believe is the major barrier to achieving excellence. If we've missed some excuses, we're more than happy to hear about them.

Second, the list is not an exercise in creative writing. These excuses, in one form or other, are what we *have been actually hearing* from education leaders at all levels and in many different kinds of schools. This is not to say that all educators and all schools are failures who wallow in destructive mediocrity. On the contrary, there are many excellent school leaders in every one of our fifty states.

These, however, are usually the people who have dealt with the problems these excuses supposedly represent, who do not tolerate a culture of excuses in their organizations, and who see any tendency to fall into the excuse trap as a call to arms. Their very success proves the point that the condition called "no more excuses" is achievable.

Finally, what we will be talking about in the next pages is not some automatic recipe or quick fix for achievement. There are no magic carpets to get us to our destination, no aircraft that can fly over thunderstorms or around mountains. This, we remind you, is a journey, not a jaunt; an expedition, not a weekend getaway. Most truly worthwhile things, of course, are always just like that.

IDEAS FOR FURTHER CONSIDERATION

It is very difficult—practically impossible, in fact—to believe that *all*, or even most of these excuses are at work in any school or school district. Many of our schools are doing very solid and effective work, and their mindset is usually directed toward educating students, not avoiding or corrupting that mission.

However, as we get ready to discuss the ways in which these excuses might be best addressed, answers to some of the following questions could serve to more realistically position your thinking about the "excuse-riddled mindset" and to what extent your own school system points toward some of its features. We recommend, if possible, that you consider the questions in serious discussion with the members of your educational team.

1. Which one or more of the seven excuses, if any, would you agree has sometimes been appealed to in some form in order to justify some particular lack of progress or failure?
2. If any of the above mentioned excuses have surfaced as a rationale for some lack of success, were there any attempts to address it in some way? Or was it regarded as an issue that could not be meaningfully undertaken, that was really out of anyone's control?

3. What would you see as the specific consequences for your school or district by not trying to address these justifications for lack of success?
4. There are many high-performing schools with great leadership and outstanding teachers and support staff. Let's assume that yours is one of them and that none of the excuses for failure are operative. Are there, nevertheless, any signs or indications that a few of these excuses might be arising, that your school is showing symptoms of vulnerability in this respect? What are those symptoms and what do you think can be done to address them?

NOTES

1. *Cultivating Leadership in Schools* (New York: Teachers College Press, 2006), 3.
2. See, for example, Fred J. Abbate, "Response to Nel Noddings's 'Excellence as a Guide to Educational Conversation,'" *Teachers College Record*, 96 no. 1 (Fall 1994) for a discussion of this approach.
3. See, for example, the reports, *The Widget Effect* published by The New Teacher Project, at www.tntp.org/ideas-and-innovations/view/the-widget-effect 2009, and *Is It Just a Bad Class?: Assessing the Stability of Measured Teacher Performance*, The Center on Reinventing Public Education Working Paper 2010–2003, University of Washington, Seattle (2010). The full report is available at www.crpe.org.

THREE
Defeating the Excuses, Part 1

Difficulty is the excuse history never accepts. —Edward R. Murrow

Well, we've now looked at the categories of excuses often used as an attempt to justify why a school or school district is failing to become anything like a high-achieving institution. In our next chapters, we will begin to offer some very specific and, we hope, some very effective ways of addressing the so-called "realities" that lead people to believe that they have no choice, that they must be "realists" and settle for much less than educational excellence. We will try to demonstrate that in most cases those "realities" are, frankly, a fraud.

THE DIRTY LITTLE SECRET IN AN EXCUSE-RIDDLED ORGANIZATION

Before we get to the specifics, however, it might be useful for us to think about the actual atmosphere—the concrete human culture—of a school or district where these excuses are accepted as unarguable fact. What is it like to work in such a school? What actually motivates the administrators, teachers, and staff to do their best? How do the students feel about what is actually going on in classrooms and about other activities?

At the root of every single one of the excuses we've described, if we think about it, is a very peculiar view of:

a. what the organization thinks about the job it has to do,
b. what the organization believes about its future,
c. what it holds to be of prime importance, and
d. how it measures genuine progress.

Put another way, an excuse-riddled culture defeats the clear and forceful sense of *mission, vision, values, and goals* ("MVVG") that high-performing organizations have, the power that unmistakably distinguishes them from second-rate, run-of-the-mill enterprises. But worse than that, to pile up excuse after excuse for consistently falling short of excellence is, in effect, to turn the school into something almost incomprehensible. Why do we say this?

Mission

Consider, for instance, the excuse that most students and parents have low expectations partnered with the excuse that teachers aren't interested in being effective educators because of tenure, and so on. Think of the logical implications of these claims. *Isn't this equivalent to saying that the very mission of the school or district has vanished? That the very reason we have education at all doesn't really exist in that school?* What business is the school in, then, if it has just about givenup completely on the teaching and learning process? Why call it a "school" at all and not, say, a meeting place for children, or (as some teachers have actually alleged) a daycare center or a babysitting operation?

Vision

If the mission is murky—or nonexistent—then what kind of future can the school and its students possibly have? Imagine a hospital, for example, that had no clear sense of what business it was in. Let's suppose it didn't see the absolute priority of caring for those who are ill and doing whatever it can to improve their health. We would, of course, have trouble even thinking of it as a hospital at all.

But, in addition, such an institution could *never* improve on what it does with new medical technology or better patient procedures simply because *what it means to improve is meaningless for it.* In short: *trying to get better at what you are not actually doing in the first place makes no sense!* Where in heaven's name would you begin? Isn't the future of such an enterprise not only fraudulent and counterfeit but almost impossible to actually imagine?

Values

All right, so a culture of excuses by its very logic entails a dubious present (mission) and a senseless future (vision). Maybe we can still rescue some of what can make it a meaningful institution. What about the things that this kind of culture truly values, for example? Isn't that still intact? Doesn't an excuse-laden school district still have a sense of solid values?

Well, unless we define the term in a very bizarre and perhaps unintelligible way, value loses all its substance in such a culture as well. Values, after all, are both what *make the mission worth pursuing* and the *guide posts that justify* why we need and want to get significantly better at pursuing the mission. Since in an excuse-laden culture both mission and vision have no clear meaning, values have to drop out of the picture. They are not just shown the exit door but kicked in the hind quarters as well.

Goals

Goals? Do goals make any sense in an excuse-riddled culture? How can working in an environment that believes it has *lost control of its very future* have any sense of needing to reach a goal? Of what possible use can the very idea of goals be in such an environment, unless they are the pedestrian aims of, say, not being annoyed or just getting through the day in one piece? And getting through the day is hardly a genuine goal; at best it's a muddled, even if sincere, wish to merely survive without too much damage.

WHERE WE GO RIGHT: THE CULTURE OF SUCCESS

Let's take a deep breath here and change the whole course of the conversation for a bit. Consider the precise contradictory of what we've been describing above.

As we have mentioned, over the past several years we have been conducting a series of seminars for education leaders called *The Academy for Education Leaders*. The leaders we work with are district superintendents and their cabinets and key administrative teams. The highly interactive sessions are designed to strengthen the participants' existing leadership capabilities and to connect them with the key elements of solid systems thinking. Our principal aim is to help these highly motivated professionals build what we call a *culture of success.*

During the program we focus on helping organizations not only understand but work to embrace the characteristics of excellence that are found in high-performing organizations. Among those characteristics are:

Authentic and Visionary Leadership
Process-Centered Thinking
A Customer-Driven Philosophy
The Commitment to Continuous Improvement
The Involvement of Everyone
Management by Fact
A Built-in Systems Perspective

What do we mean by a culture of success? It is the culture that is found in any high-performing organization, whether it's a manufacturing plant, a trucking company, a hospital, a football team, and, yes, even a school and school district. No doubt, anyone can guess that it involves the exact opposite of the culture of excuses we've been describing so far. And though true, there is much more to say about it, for the insightful research done over years by people like John Kotter at Harvard, Jeffrey Pfeffer at Stanford, Michael Fullan at the University of Toronto, Jim Collins, Warren Bennis, and many others has shown us some pretty solid things.[1]

First, they are organizations that *successfully respond to change*, no matter where the change comes from. To meet any challenge they confront, they engage the talents of their people as a quintessential resource. They put a great deal of emphasis on getting, keeping, developing, and motivating the very best people they can possibly find. In short, they have a high-commitment approach to human resources, not only to financial or other kinds of resources. They manage risk by relying on their people.

In addition, these talented people are not thought of as individual performers, but as team members who work together for a common cause and outcome. As Warren Bennis tells us, they're characterized as Great Groups who focus like lasers and believe they are on a mission from God to get the most important things done.

Next, in high-performing organizations there is a *sense of unadulterated optimism* that is built into their very culture, into the very day-to-day operations of the business, a sense that nothing is too difficult to be accomplished no matter what the risk, a clear idea of who the "enemy" is. The enemy could be a competitor, or ignorance, or indifference, or an economic downturn. There is also a sense that the work being done is worth doing for its own sake and is in large part its own reward. Excuses are *not ever* part of the picture for these enterprises.

Third, these organizations have a clear and palpable *aversion to anything that even resembles bureaucracy*. When less successful companies make organizational changes, they often just substitute one bureaucratic structure for another one—a way of seeming to take a risk without actually doing anything at all. Real high-performance companies minimize such structures, generally in the name of teamwork, partnership, and trust. In these organizations, you hear more talk about "coalitions" than you do about departments, more about "task forces" than divisions, and you find them celebrating the success of groups just as much as they celebrate increases to the bottom line.

High-performing organizations not only react and respond to change, as we've said, but they deliberately *seek it out and encourage more of it*. While certainly respecting the core values and fully understanding the worth of the tactics and strategies that have worked in the past, these organizations are constantly *challenging the status quo* and the prevailing wisdom, things that keep us tied to a false sense of comfort because the future has so much uncertainty built into it. These successful organizations are usually and systematically scanning the environment for new trends, different waves, and shifts in the wind. They make future risk less threatening by understanding their present not as events moving into the past but moving into the future. They seek to know what that future means and what it implies for the introduction of new systems and procedures.

In addition, the most successful high-performance organizations are very clear about what specifically counts as progress and what does not. In short, they are *data-driven organizations* that emphasize relevant measures of improvement, enterprises that do not rely on "gut feel" or intuition, but enterprises that constantly manage by fact. They never confuse mere activity with action, mere expenditure of energy with progress. The mantra of these organizations is: *Plan-Do-Check-Act*. (We will say more about this mantra in later discussions.) They keep asking: What do we do? For whom do we do it? How are we doing? And how do we know that we're doing it well?

THE CRITICAL ROLE OF LEADERSHIP: PERFORMING THE TRUTH

None of these-high performance characteristics would be possible or even conceivable without the most crucial attribute on which they all depend, namely, effective leadership. The leadership of these organizations constantly, consistently, and relentlessly communicates a clear, unmistakable vision of what the organization must aspire to be. The vision is not the same as the mission, as we've seen above, which describes the business you are in. The vision of effective leaders outlines what Jim Collins, in his book *Good to Great,* calls the "BHAG"—the big, hairy, audacious goal; the vision is about not simply how you can be good, not simply how you can be better, but how you can be *the best in the world at what you do*.

These are leaders who get results from others by example and not mere words, and who steadfastly and uncompromisingly keep the entire organization focused on a shared, meaningful vision. Leaders take risks, push the probability envelope, and welcome the chance to deal with any impacts that might result.

Effective leaders are, by definition, change agents. They are committed to lead in ways that are always looking for change, always seeking to move closer to increased quality and greater achievement. There has been a lot written about leadership in the past few years—much of it sounding more and more like psychotherapy and spiritualism—but it really boils down to this: *leaders are people who redefine risk as opportunity and convincingly get that message established throughout the entire organization.*

As a result, they are the vital backbone of these high-performing enterprises, whether they are major corporations, small businesses, or school districts. They are the key reasons these organizations have turned the risks associated with change into opportunities for building a solid culture of success. Effective leaders do not rely on excuses, and do not seek out individuals or groups to blame. They seek the *real causes* of why something isn't up to the right standards by demonstrating a continuous questioning spirit—and urging such a spirit throughout the organization.

If he or she is a school superintendent or a principal, there is never any doubt among teachers and other staff that raising questions about the status quo is valued and encouraged. In this way, in fact, they are helping others to become leaders themselves; their followers are not disciples who have squandered their autonomy but who understand its value. The freedom, creativity, and innovation of everyone in the organization—no matter what their tasks—are among the leader's highest values.

Successful leaders constantly lead through moral character and are seldom guilty of the self-deception that arrogance generates. They avoid "playing the role" of leader or confusing leadership with a "power trip" or authority trap. Their focus is on testing assumptions by the logic of results, including their own performance. The best leaders, to put it in a phrase, are action-oriented. Leaders do not push and they do not pull; they lead. Truth is what they value most, but not only the truth of words or statements. *They lead by performing the truth and do not simply utter it.* And they perform and embody the truth in just about everything they do.

But there is no rapid road or quick fix to being an effective leader. Leadership requires making connections, making relationships, and like any relationship worth having—friendship, love, marriage, partnering, parenting—it needs constant hard work, constant renewal, constant maintenance. As Warren Bennis keeps reminding us, *Great Groups and Great Leaders create each other*, just as all relationships require involvement and commitment by the parties involved. There are times when it goes wrong, as happens to even the best leaders, and there are times when one gets it exactly right. And, yes, there are bound to be those times when leaders aren't quite sure whether they've gotten it right or wrong.

AUTHENTIC LEADERSHIP

Above almost every other characteristic, effective leaders are *authentic* leaders. Think about it. The leaders who stand apart from others are the ones about whom we have no doubt that they are the real thing, not acting a role or, worse, enjoying the power the role gives them. In our Academy for Education Leaders we stress this genuineness as a critical feature in our model of what we call the *Lessons of Authentic Leadership*. The model might serve to both summarize and expand on some of the concepts we've been discussing. It does not take a great deal of analysis to see that the lessons are thoroughly connected with each other. And that is because authentic leadership requires all of them to be fully at work.

The discussion of the model could be a very productive one for you and your key team members after you review it and check your own practice in light of its elements. In fact, we urge you to schedule several collaborative dialogues about it as soon as you can.

THE EIGHT LESSONS OF AUTHENTIC LEADERSHIP

Lesson 1: Discriminate Between Surface and Substance

(a) Develop a continuous questioning spirit

Leaders do not accept the logic of the "prevailing winds" in an organization. On the contrary, they seek constantly to *get to the bottom* of issues, even when those prevailing winds are considered sacrosanct in the or-

Figure 3.1.

ganization. As we've already seen, the inability to differentiate between what is real and what only appears to be real lies at the very heart of the excuse-riddled mentality. This lesson does not imply questioning for its own sake, which seldom gets anyone anywhere. It is rather the honest examination and analysis of the institutional positions and long-standing practices that might or might not still have validity. (We're told that Mark Twain declared that sacred cows make the best hamburgers.)

This lesson also underscores why bureaucracy is always looked upon in high-performing organizations with suspicion, since the pronouncements of "officialdom" are generally wrapped with a cloak of authority that does not invite questions. That cloak usually hides the fact that the practice has no rationale for it other than the comforting feeling of what has always been done.

(b) Foster that spirit throughout the organization

Leaders who genuinely matter and who keep aiming for first-class results promote, cultivate, and consistently encourage this kind of thinking at every level of the enterprise. The do this by setting the example of the questioning spirit. If leaders' actions contradict their words, those whom they presume to lead will *always* follow the actions, for the words have been shown to be meaningless. Effective leaders over and over again demonstrate that they value the questioning spirit of their colleagues, for by raising such questions they are interested in achieving what is best for the organization.

Of course, if you must foster a questioning spirit throughout your school district, you must also be clearly and transparently committed to taking those questions seriously, to answering and dealing with those questions honestly, and, above all, to avoid suspecting the motives behind them. In organizations of all types that consistently value challenging the accepted wisdom, the only motive ascribed to anyone who questions a practice or policy is this: they are sincerely seeking to make the organization better in some way.

Yes, there might be times when something else, some "hidden agenda" could be at work, but the evidence shows pretty well that if you encourage questions and treat the inquiries people make as honestly motivated attempts to improve the enterprise, more often than not that will be the motive you will get. It's no secret that we often get what we expect to get in many departments of life.

Lesson 2: Confront the Likelihood of Self-deception

(a) Distinguish between vision and hallucination

Connected with Lesson 1, true leaders regularly assess their own values, motives, and intentions when they act or make decisions so that they can be sure they are acting for the good of the enterprise and not from some other aim, whether conscious or not. Effective leaders, we have said, set a clear, challenging, and strong vision for the organization. They must, however, regularly check to be sure that their vision is something truly shared and inspiring for all in the organization, not some personal and eccentric mental picture that others can neither understand nor act upon because they can't quite find the handles on it.

Now, we all sometimes tell pretty good stories to ourselves about ourselves and hold to the purity of our intentions. Even the best leaders can sometimes fall into the trap of self-deception. That is why it is critically important to think about our decisions by putting them to the test of fact, not wish fulfillment. The key question to ask is, "On what facts is my judgment based? How much of what I am recommending to those who report to me is a result of how I feel and how much based upon what I have data to support?" If you actually write down you answers to make them visible, the illumination can be impressive, even dazzling at times.

Leaders in education especially need to find ways to celebrate the achievements of those who are doing things that get the school district closer to the vision, to what the district genuinely aspires to be or become. We have noticed, unfortunately, that many of the educational leaders we have worked with do not celebrate real achievements often enough. This sometimes can be due to the mistaken belief that praising a person can somehow lead to a decrease of his or her effort in future projects.

This "Attila the Hun" theory of managing people has got things upside down. For, on the contrary, if the celebration is for a genuine and meaningful result that contributes to the positive future of the organization, it will commonly lead to *even more* effort in subsequent assignments. Of course, if one praises for everything and anything, then it won't take long before the process has lost all significance, and the leader's credibility is doomed.

We'll explore some further points about visions in our last chapter.

(b) Settle only for facts, not mythology

Every organization has its own version of mythic stories and particular folklore about its practices and policies. Sometimes these imply the belief that things are going extremely well in a particular area, or the opposite, namely, that things are a disaster in a department or region of the enterprise. Effective and authentic leadership always wants to know on *what facts such judgments are based*, and does not simply accept the mere perpetuation of these beliefs as gospel written in stone.

To evaluate any performance, whether of people, processes, or systems, requires data, factual information, not simply feelings or unsubstantiated convictions. Although these feelings might be strongly and widely held, they are usually uninspected and more often than not can actually stand as obstacles in the way of the truth, the very information that is essential for the productive future of the organization.

We should not underestimate the powerful hold organizational myths and traditions have on even the best enterprises. They can function like the unconscious perceptions of reality that affect individual minds. And even when laid bare and seen for what they actually are, many heads of even major businesses are reluctant to challenge them outright. People in the organization, as we have already seen, often consider the positive versions of the folklore to be the unspoken and long-standing values holding the operation together. And when you cross pollinate this view with the normal resistance to change that human beings seem to bring to any activity or process, the need to move cautiously and not threateningly becomes clear.

Lesson 3: Lead through Moral Character

(a) Solid values are essential to integrity

"Don't worry about actually being honest in politics," an old joke has it, "just make sure you do your very best to fake it."

Authentic leadership can't be faked, no matter how good an actor one might be, because, as we noted above, in the longer run leaders are evaluated by how they act, not by what they say. Perhaps in contemporary politics the faker is more difficult to spot, since politicians have at their disposals media consultants, communications experts, spin doctors, and sometimes more than enough money to give their constituents the appearance of genuine action. But the values that are part and parcel of a leader's very makeup determine, like all values, the kinds of things the leader seeks to embody in everything she or he does. Lack of integrity, in short, will eventually become observable to those whom one is charged with leading.

Some studies of leadership have implied that we can learn a great deal even from the evil leaders of the past and present—a Hitler or a Stalin, for example—since their techniques for getting others to follow can serve as interesting case studies for us.[2] Yet it should be perfectly clear that we truly have nothing of value to learn from such people, since, even if we might realize the effectiveness of their cunning ability and rhetorical style, we see that such skills are hollow without the moral fiber to back them.

And that is why we could not ever seriously admire them. They treated those in their charge as mere means to their own evil ends, not as centers of intrinsic value deserving of respect. Authentic leaders *value persons as persons* and never as mere instruments for their selfish ends. Authentic leaders are moral leaders and, therefore, never accomplish results by playing on the fears of those whom they are obligated to lead and lead well.

(b) Without integrity you cannot have credibility

This key point is a simple but extremely powerful one. Effective leadership has to be consistently *believable* leadership.[3] No one follows the leadership of anyone suspected of being a fraud or a liar. The person of integrity is a person of principle, and moral principle is at the very heart of credibility. Note that moral principle is *not the same a moralizing*. In fact, the moralizer who persistently preaches his or her own beliefs as if they were revealed from on high will seldom be an effective leader, because the moralizing signals superiority. Great leaders, like Harriet Tubman, whose integrity was strikingly exemplified in her actions of getting slaves to freedom, do not give speeches and recite platitudes. By the nature of their commitments and actions, their essential moral character is revealed without question.

Lesson 4: Make New Leaders, Not Disciples

(a) Bring out the right stuff in your people

Tom Wolfe's fascinating book of some years ago about the training and exceptional skill of American astronauts was, many will remember, entitled *The Right Stuff* for the very good reason that these very special people had what it takes to get one of the most difficult jobs we've ever imagined done exceptionally well. The book's title should be a watchword for every leader, since the leader's effectiveness depends critically and literally on *making leaders out of followers*.

These astronauts had extraordinary training, had total support from superiors to succeed whenever it was needed, and were given autonomy for the awesome responsibility to complete ground-breaking missions. The great Chinese philosopher Lao Tzu is reported to have said, "If the leader has done his job well, those he leads will say we have done it ourselves." This, to our way of thinking, is one of the biggest secrets of successful leadership, namely, that *the authentic leader does not only respect followers' autonomy, but persistently fosters, consistently encourages, and vigorously supports the greater development of that autonomy.*

The lesson is a difficult thing to learn for some of the educational and other leaders we have worked with, for the simple reason that there appears something paradoxical—maybe even contradictory—about it. Aren't followers, one might ask, supposed to act like followers? And the answer is, yes, but *the leader is not a guru*, not the anointed champion who has some special conduit to the truth denied to mere mortals. And followers are not the leader's disciples whose entire value and purpose are determined by being slavish and submissive servants. This view of leadership wears away genuine innovation and vision-directed action in those whom one must lead. It also treats followers as only a means to someone else's ends. This is the very antithesis of the moral perspective, and that makes it the antithesis of bona fide leadership itself.

(b) Do not stuff your people full of right

Authentic leaders understand and regularly signal that they do not simply *want* meaningful engagement by everyone in the team they lead. They constantly signal that such engagement *is absolutely essential* to the success of the team. In short, the best leaders never send a message that in any way suggests that they have all the answers, have a corner on the market of wisdom, are the smartest ones in the room. On the contrary, they find ways to emphasize that they need the help of others who will most assuredly have ideas that they never thought of. Jim Collins in *Good to Great* calls this "Level 5 Leadership," the level whose distinctive characteristic is genuine humility.

Again, this is a concept that goes down with some difficulty for many in leadership positions, whether they be CEOs of large organizations or supervisors in a local nonprofit. One of the recurrent glitches that showed up when companies began introducing quality-improvement teams in the 1980s was that the traditional supervisors sometimes felt threatened by not having all the answers, by hearing ideas they never thought of.

It was a short jump from that feeling to the conclusion that their leadership itself was in decline and that their careers were soon going to show up on the discount shelf. Perhaps the problems were mostly a result of how we trained supervisors and managers for so many years, stressing the concept of being "in charge." We tended to confuse leadership with control *over others*, not as the practice of encouraging the thoughts and behavior of those others to do their very best. "No one of us," an important saying goes, "is smarter than all of us." (We'll revisit this maxim later; it really can't be overstated.)

Lesson 5: Promote True Freedom and Innovation

(a) Good people have good ideas

Leaders must constantly work using the premise that in general people want to do good work, want to get better at their jobs, and that they value the freedom to decide on the best ways to get great results from the work they do. In organizations where leaders bring out this kind of "right stuff" in their colleagues, the atmosphere is palpably different from those where autonomy and freedom are not valued. You can often feel it just as you walk in the door, whether it's a mega supermarket or a small business. These organizations more often show not only the spirit, but the reality of fresh approaches to old problems, new product and market ideas, increased productivity, and an evident sense of energy and exhilaration.

In the higher-performing schools where we have worked, the same atmospheric differences can be immediately seen and felt by anyone visiting the building. There is an enthusiasm and animation on the faces and in the movements of everyone—students, teachers, and support staff. At almost every level and in almost every case, the people involved believe that they are valued as people, not as mere means to someone else's end.

(b) Only good ideas have good consequences

This point might appear to be a tautology, but it is really a reminder that our reason to nourish good ideas from good people lies in the productive outcomes they give us. If leadership is to be truly authentic, then is must eliminate from its consciousness the destructive idea that it is about being liked, being nice, being a "Regular Person." Of course, leaders need to be admired and respected if they are to lead effectively, but the best leaders are the ones who get the *right* things done, not simply the *nice* things done. Leading is about performance, and we evaluate performance by its outcomes.

Again, we have met our share of business leaders and school officials who have, perhaps unconsciously, adopted the view that leading is really about not upsetting the apple cart—a kind of "Don't Ask, Don't Tell" approach. As a result, they expect harmony because they demand nothing. When you think a bit longer about this style, however, you realize that it really signals a lack of respect for those the leader is charged with leading.

One assistant superintendent demonstrated the point most clearly and depressingly. When he was asked if the administration had sought the views of teachers when developing a new curriculum design, he responded that they had not. The reason? He was very concerned that the teachers were bound to have ideas that he could not implement. That would lead to disappointment, and the teachers would conclude that he had no respect for them. It never occurred to him that the lack of respect for the teaching staff was the original premise on which he was acting in the first place.

Lesson 6: Test Your Assumptions by the Logic of Results

(a) Never measure the water's depth with both feet

The reason why good leaders want to constantly keep stirring a questioning spirit in the teams they lead is, among other things, to make sure that decisions made by the organization are based on solid, tested data. Even the best and brightest of scientists can sometimes unconsciously become attached to a "pet" hypothesis. As a result they might look only for data that confirms what they wanted to believe in the first place.

It is important, therefore, to make sure that the data is not selected only to substantiate one side of the story, but that we deliberately look for facts that might prove our assumption wrong. And, as we've seen, this same warning has to apply to any enterprise, whether a school, a hospital, or a multinational corporation. The tendency to resort to rationalization when what we already believe doesn't cohere with new facts is, clearly, just another excuse story. Our students did not do well on a state test? Well, it must be a dreadful test. The incidents of absenteeism in our schools are on the increase? It must be the increased use of video games and/or other technologies that make learning seem too boring to participate in.

We are told that there is a Native American piece of advice on this score: "Never test the depth of the water with both feet." Of course, in the actual case of doing this, you are apt to put your very life at risk. But assumptions about what facts are truly relevant to your beliefs can be almost as dangerous to many more people than yourself, namely, those who depend on your leadership. To keep the water metaphor going, we might add: "The policy of jumping in with both feet is no smart way to get to the bottom of things."

(b) Live in the real world with a really open mind

Leadership, we know, crucially requires a visionary approach to the future, a view of the world that stresses new and revitalizing possibilities, rather than one that sees more of what the comfortable present keeps showing us. To some people of a slightly more pessimistic psyche, this feature of good leadership might seem to be just a hopeless version of Pollyannaism. "Get real!" one might hear them say; the world isn't your—or anyone else's—oyster, and when things go wretchedly wrong, you will have more disappointment than loyalty among your followers.

This objection, however, misses an important point. Being an authentic leader with a strong vision does not, as we've been saying, involve building castles in the clouds. A vision is what an organization aspires to become, given its mission, values, and goals, and the inspiration of that vision actually reinforces the strength of those key elements. A school system that aspires to become one of the best in the state, for example, begins to reanimate its mission, to redirect its goals, and to make its core values much more powerfully conscious.

These then become more operative and more effective in everything it does. It would be absurd for a school district to, say, aspire to become the best provider of health care services in the state, just as much as it would be ridiculous for a trucking company to aim to become the foremost library in the state. Visions are connected to the mission, talents, and interests of those for whom the vision serves as the magnet drawing us toward excellence. The best leaders know this, which is why you hear them stress the power of the vision by using it as the framework to measure new and old policies and practices. This is their "real world." What can sometimes pass for "realism" in organizations with low expectations is just another excuse for not improving.

Lesson 7: Avoid Power Trips and Authority Traps

(a) Don't confuse your title with your leadership

This point perhaps needs very little explanation, since many of us at one time or other surely and unfortunately have encountered people with grandiose titles but the weakest of leadership skills. Yet, it is easy to understand the temptation to confuse the implications of the label with the reality of the contents, for we have already explored how self-deception is a real threat to a leader's effectiveness.

If I have been promoted to vice president, superintendent, principal, or some other designation, I can reason that the promotion was either fully deserved or somehow unjustified. Barring total cynicism as a way of life, the latter conclusion, of course, hardly makes for a meaningful self-concept. I need to generally believe that my new title reflects in some significant way my capabilities, not some accident that occurred without any reason. Authentic leaders, however, while acknowledging their official title, believe it is only a means to getting significant things accomplished for the organization and the people in it. No title is self-justified for an effective leader. It is only an *opportunity* to achieve much more important objectives. This is also part of the "real world" leaders must live in.

(b) All power, we know in our hearts, tends to corrupt

Lord Acton's famous quotation—"Power corrupts and absolute power corrupts absolutely"—should always serve as one of the major adages of good leadership. Leadership, we have been saying in so many ways and from so many perspectives, is not about power, except, perhaps, the power to set solid examples for others. Authentic leadership is constantly seeking better approaches to building leaders, valuing collaborative practices by action, not by mere words, and trusting those who are being led to do the right thing.

Leaders are empowered by those whom they lead precisely because they empower others. And if this sounds paradoxical or even contradictory, then one needs to reflect more on the true role of leadership. Power, after all, implies control, and control of others entails that those others are not allowed to exercise genuine freedom and innovation. Small wonder, then, that power corrupts leadership, and those who relish having power over others will never be in the same league as the authentic leader.

Lesson 8: Do not Simply Utter the Truth—Perform It!

(a) Your true native language is Action

It might seem a little strange to talk about *performing* the truth. We do not ordinarily speak about truth this way, since we associate truth with statements or beliefs we have. What we have in mind here, however, can be seen by thinking about the way we might describe someone as a "true" friend or distinguish a "true" diamond from a fake one, or say that a novel has "the ring of truth" about it. Truth in this sense means "authenticity," as opposed to something artificial or phony.

We have been describing effective leaders by the ways in which they act, not by the ways in which they speak. Authentic leaders perform the truth by exhibiting—in practice and in performance—the values, attitudes, beliefs, and principles that show them to be the real thing. Leaders who matter, in short, do not simply add the truth to their performance; the truth infuses every aspect of how they act. This is the real language they constantly speak to us, why we trust them and why we believe their leadership matters to us.

(b) In the end, leaders must actually lead!

Authentic leaders get their results through others, not in isolation from them. They perform with others, not at the expense of others. Those who depend on the leader must always *be better off for having followed* than by doing otherwise. And those on whom the followers depend—especially, in the case of the educational enterprise, students who are put into their charge—will be better for it as well.

CHALLENGING THE GHOSTS OF THE PAST

In the next chapter, as we've pointed out, we'll begin to address the particular kinds of excuses that were unpacked earlier. Unless our administrators, teachers, and boards of education come to understand that the justifications for the excuses are generally false and perniciously invented, the possibility of achieving a culture of success in our schools cannot move one inch from square one. We have learned this critical lesson from working with educators at all levels.

But what we have also learned is that without authentic educational leadership, *leadership that is committed to eliminating the excuse culture in all of its manifestations*, the ways of addressing the excuses will and cannot last. Just as there is no royal road to effective leadership, so there is no quick and easy way to fix difficult problems of long-standing and wide-ranging consequences. Authentic, effective leadership is what gives a school and school district permanent, consistent, and standardized solutions, a culture that makes success the rule and not the exception.

There is a critical need for innovative leadership in education, for new and more meaningful ways of holding our schools accountable for measurable results while still respecting the creativity and professionalism of those who manage them. There is a need for shedding the straightjackets of bureaucracy, the myth that education cannot learn from the excellence in the leadership and operations found in other fields, and for building an atmosphere that never, ever rewards the litany of excuses that turn people into victims.

The difficulty here is worth repeating. *Leaders, we've said, redefine risk as opportunity.* There will always be barriers and roadblocks to overcome or get around on any given day in our schools. They can be overcome. But committing to high-performance and to effective leadership means committing to the long haul. The literature is filled with stories of companies who thought they could make the move in one swift overnight leap, that they could announce a new direction or strategic focus, and expect that everyone would jump on the train and happily sojourn into the Promised Land.

But successful organizations and their leaders understand that meaningful change takes time; it has none of the elements of a show down at the O.K. Corral. Whether you're in the education business or the utility business or the trucking business or trying to win the Stanley Cup, the movement to excellence requires that gains be made slowly, if the gains are to be real and really worth celebrating. Be pleased about the small wins you achieve, but understand that they are only steps in a long process.

Take another very big, deep breath. In the next chapter we will take aim and start addressing the specific litany of excuses.

IDEAS FOR FURTHER CONSIDERATION

A few questions might help focus some discussion of these lessons of leadership.

1. To what degree do you see them at work in your own day-to-day leadership?
2. When you reflect on the leaders you have admired, either in your own actual experience or in cases you have read about, can you identify any examples of these practices exhibited in the behavior of those leaders?
3. If there are areas in these lessons that are not part of your own regular leader behavior, or practices that might even exhibit tendencies that contradict them, what do you believe might be the causes of those difficulties?
4. Some leaders who have identified areas for further development have sought the advice of colleagues whose leadership they admire, have enrolled in courses or special seminars on leadership, or have done some additional reading on research-based leadership practices; we will have some suggestions later on. If there are areas for further development that you believe need improvement, how might you plan to go about addressing them?
5. Keep this point in mind, no matter where you are with respect to the leadership lessons: they are not a recipe for a completed project. No leader is ever finished becoming a better leader, just as no one is ever finished learning anything worthwhile. To lead is to be connected with others in some very special and often very complicated ways, and those others will always find something new for a leader to react to and to grow from.

Note: In our Appendix following the last chapter in this volume, you'll have a chance to do a self-assessment on your own leadership authenticity.

NOTES

1. For these and other valuable references, see the "Leaders and High-Performing Organizations" bibliography in the Appendix.
2. Howard Garner's excellent study of these techniques in his *Leading Minds: An Anatomy of Leadership* (New York: Basic Books, 1995), does not, of course, support leading like these and other tyrants. But his treating them as subjects as valuable to look at as Gandhi or Pope John XXIII does not stress the moral dimension of leadership. As a psychologist he is, no doubt, abstracting from this feature in order to be as descriptive as the mental terrain allows.
3. See *Credibility*, James M. Kouzes and Barry Z. Posner (San Francisco: Jossey-Bass, 1993) for first-rate work on this point.

FOUR

Defeating the Excuses, Part 2

If you don't want to do something, one excuse is as good as another.
—Yiddish Proverb

THE EXCUSES EXAMINED

First Excuse: "You just don't get our problem!"

Reply: "You might be right. Tell me about it in a way that I can understand."

The reply above, no doubt, sounds pretty glib. Perhaps it is, but it is really the most important opening response that one can give in this kind of educational conversation. For the "problem" that is at issue is not one thing but a collection of things. And if the person who replies fails to understand your problem it is most likely a case of your not describing it in any meaningful way.

But much more significant is this: you tell us that your problems are unique, that the solutions to problems facing other kinds of enterprises just won't work in education. Do you actually and fully understand your own problems? *Have you described your problems meaningfully even to yourself and to the professionals in your school district?* Or are you just content to take pleasure in their ambiguity and keep using them as an excuse for inaction?

First of all, every school, like every complex organization, has lots of problems. Some are not difficult ones and can be dealt with pretty handily or even left on the back burner for a while. Others, however, are extremely significant, and unless the causes are found and addressed can have (and probably are already having) damaging and perhaps even toxic effects on the operations, mission, values, and goals of your district. These are the high-priority, front burner problems, the ones that must be addressed and fixed if your schools are ever going to get close to building a culture of excellence. Let's get this problem out in the open and see if the tools used by other kinds of organizations could work to help address it.

So here's your first issue. What is the most important problem facing your district right now? Which thing do you absolutely *need* to improve on—not just *want* to improve on? Tell yourself as clearly as you can about this Godzilla-like issue, the issue that simply *has to be addressed* and (perhaps) that everyone in the district has been avoiding as if it doesn't actually exist—like the proverbial elephant in the room.

The critical part of the battle you are going to fight with this problem is getting it described correctly and meaningfully in the first place. And this is not as easy as it might seem, given our experience working with many organizations, including school leaders and their key support groups. It just won't do, for example, to list these kinds of problems for attention and action:

"Things are just a mess around here."
"We've had growing morale problems over the past years."
"Student achievement is not what it should be."
"We are failing to communicate at all levels."

All of these might be true in some sense, but in the murky form in which they are expressed, one just doesn't know what to possibly *do* about them or where to start getting a useful handle on them. Some important guidelines have to be used to make the description of the problem—what we're going to call the Problem Statement—something we can work with. A doctor keeps trying to get as much detail as she can about the patient's symptoms precisely so that finding the cause becomes a more accurate enterprise and can be correctly addressed. And that is the same case here.

The guidelines for a problem statement are the first of several critical tools you will need in order to make significant progress. We'll revisit problem statements in the next chapter, because we believe there is never enough to say about their importance. The participants in our Academy for Education Leaders often have more difficulty with this tool than any other, as do corporate and other executives we have worked with.

A useful and actionable problem statement must, we will argue later, require much more specificity, be objectively stated, show some way of measuring the scope of the problem, and point out the gap to be bridged by addressing the issue. (The acronym for this will be *SMOG*, but more on that in our next chapter.) So statements such as "Things are going down the drain fast around here" do not even arise to the level of a problem, since one doesn't know where to begin addressing them. What, in short, is anyone supposed to do about this so-called problem? What consequential actions are we to pursue? What facts or data do we need to collect and analyze in order to address it?

So let's look generally at our first excuse again and see if we've gained anything so far. We don't understand your problem or problems, we are told? The real question is: *do you understand your problems?* The only way to understand your problem so that we can address it is to state it in an *actionable way*.

Several consequential things are possible when you do this.

First, of the many problems you might think you should address, you are now able to see which of them has the higher priority. A high dropout rate in your school is going to clearly seem a lot more important than, say, a rise in the cost of janitorial supplies. True, you might have several important issues on your plate, but you cannot—*you must not*—try to address them all at the same time, any more than a sharpshooter can try to hit multiple targets at the exact same time. One way to analyze priorities is to rate the issues against three criteria. Suppose you're trying to decide whether problem A or B is the higher priority.

- Which one is more serious? Which problem is having the most significant impact on our mission, vision, values, and goals?
- Which one is more imperative and needs to be handled without loss of time?
- Which one will get worse and grow more difficult to manage if left alone?

The second thing writing an effective and actionable problem statement can do for you is put you and your staff in the best position to find the root cause, the real cause of the problem. "Things are a mess around here" and other similar claims are really just vague expressions of frustration about which nothing can be done—except, perhaps, sympathy, or pity. (We'll discuss finding the root cause later.)

The third thing you gain from putting your problem statement in the right order is this: you now can see that there is no substantive or procedural difference in the problems educators face and the problems hospitals, manufacturers, and airlines face. Yes, they are about different things and involve different people, but the process by which we can get a good grip on them is really no different. Yes, you and your educational experts know more about addressing them than people outside of your business, but—guess what—we can now actually understand what you're trying to do after all. What's more important? So can you.

So much for your first excuse. But stay with us. We'll have a lot more to say about it later.

Second Excuse: "Students just aren't interested in learning."

Reply: "Maybe it isn't exactly learning they're turning away from."

There's an old joke among stand-up comics. There are two comedians talking:

First comedian: "How'd did your show go last night?"

Second comedian: "Not too well."

First comedian: "That's too bad. What do you think happened?"

Second comedian: "Oh, I *know* what happened! I was just too smart for the room."

This is a classic example of a Blame Game, where the fault is not in what we are doing but in those for whom we are trying to do it. A manufacturer whose product is not selling very well would be extremely foolish to conclude that the product is too high in quality for the customers.[1] And, of course, as we mentioned earlier, putting the blame as far outside of oneself as possible is a perfect way to avoid responsibility for making any changes and to avoid looking into the true reasons why the failure happened.

In the student case, we jump to the parents, to the culture, to the impact of television, texting, iPads, video games, and so on. But jumping to any of these causes, or any combination of them and others we might dream up, has absolutely no clear meaning unless we have first asked some relevant questions. And, in fact, these are exactly the questions that high-performing school districts have asked and have worked hard to get answers to:

- How do we actually know that students aren't interested, that is, *on the basis of what data* or evidence can this claim be supported? And if you are correct, what gives you the license to jump to a particular cause without data?

There are two issues here for openers. First, how many students are we talking about? All? Some? Most? Many? Are you painting a few with the broad and fallacious brush of overgeneralization? Second, lack of interest covers a very wide territory, of course, and to make the claim that students, no matter how many, and, perhaps, parents have lost all sense of the importance of education is already to have landed on a very specific interpretation. Certain kinds of behaviors can be indicative of several different things. But even if the claim is correct, why leave it at that? Surely there has to be a cause for the symptom, and if you think the likely candidates are television or social media or anything else, you have to justify the claim.

- Have we seriously endeavored to engage students with help in envisioning their futures and identifying their key operational and life values?

The manufacturer mentioned above whose products aren't selling is most likely someone who never seriously thought about finding out what customers want or need. Surveys, of course, are one way of finding such things out, but the best way is to partner such surveys with active and honest engagement of customers, get them to act with you in a spirit of cooperation and collaboration so that both provider and consumer are connecting with each other at the right level and about the right things.

Students need the same kind of involvement. Repeated studies over many years have found that one of the biggest deterrents to student interest is that they do not see a genuine connection between what goes on in the classroom and what future they see for themselves. Many students, no doubt, are not clear about that future, and might even structure it for themselves in a negative way, that is, in terms of knowing what they do not ever want to do.[2] But the schools and school districts that have many of their students totally energized about learning are those that help students clarify their values, honor those values, and work hard at showing how education can address a future that embodies those values.

- Have we got a clear idea about what we *would count as genuine progress* for students? More importantly, are students involved in evaluating their own progress?

Long-standing and hallowed tradition has put the teacher in the role of sole and, often, isolated evaluator of how students are achieving. While not denying that this role is an important one, high-performing schools involve students in assessing their own progress in significant ways. Obviously, we are not suggesting that this is a policy that works with children in the early grades, yet even here there is room for some creative approaches. For middle- and high-school students, when we clearly show them that we expect them not only to be high achievers but to appraise themselves meaningfully on how they are progressing, this policy has great payoff.

At the very least, it offers wonderful opportunities for a *genuinely collaborative* approach to grades and portfolio assessment. For another, it makes evaluation about persons, not bloodless numbers on a score sheet. Physicians tell us that the best patients are the ones who understand that they have to take some control of their own health, not act as merely passive recipients of doctoring. Great corporations and nonprofits also know that employee and customer engagement makes for the highest probabilities for success. So it should be with our students.

- Are we doing anything substantive to help teachers to discover their most effective teaching styles? Are we doing anything to help students discover their own learning styles?

Here again we have not done nearly enough in our American educational practices or educator training on this score, generally relying on a one-size-fits-all approach to learning and teaching and, perhaps, believing that style is not as important as what's in a standard curriculum or test protocol. In our work with educational leaders, we stress the critical need to address the factors in our personalities and values that help or hinder our readiness, enthusiasm, and interest in what is trying to be delivered in any human communicative activity. As we noted earlier, the more we involve our students and our teachers in structured and systematic dialogue about life and operational values, the better we will be able to make clear progress on getting the right things across in the right way.

- What are we doing to work with everyone in the school district to get a better picture for how we can improve and how to measure it?

We'll say more about this in the analysis of a later excuse, but it should be pretty obvious by now that the significance of involving students and teachers in meaningful ways will also apply to major stakeholders in the districts—parents, community leaders, political and social decision makers.

The questions we have posed above are not merely theoretical niceties. Asking them honestly and moving methodically, carefully, and comprehensively to address them can work and can make for considerable improvement not only for student achievement, but for building a culture that settles for nothing less than success. We have worked with schools and school districts that have made solid and quantifiable progress in addressing the questions of lack of student interest.

In one school in particular, the lack of interest was shown by overtly negative student behavior that seem to be increasing weekly. Huge improvement occurred by everyone working collaboratively and cooperatively in addressing these and related questions and the ones answers gave rise to. But whether the symptoms are growing absenteeism or low parental involvement, they can be addressed and clear progress can be made and made to last.

Think about this: if we conclude (a) that students and parents have no possible appreciation for the value of education, and (b) there is nothing that anyone can do about it, *then there is simply no point in trying to deliver it.* And from that conclusion it clearly follows, as we noted earlier on in these pages, that the mission, vision, values, and goals of the educational enterprise have lost any meaning they might have had. To talk about improving it, therefore, is a patently foolish errand. And this is an errand, of course, that is headed nowhere.

Third Excuse: "Our community doesn't support us; it's probably against us!"

Reply: "Have you tired communicating with the community? We don't mean talking; we mean *really communicating*."

Let's start by reiterating one of the key points we made a bit ago.[3] It might certainly be the case that a school district has some genuine and even serious difficulty with the community. A district we worked with had such tensions with the town's citizenry, and the administrators knew full well that the issue was a significant one. There were numerous complaints coming into the superintendent's office and almost weekly letters to the local newspapers about everything from bad teachers to the rising costs of school taxes. School personnel were constantly approached with questions and negative comments no matter where they walked in town.

The significant point here is this: this district *did not use the difficulty as an excuse* to fold up its tent and hike off into the barren desert of futility. On the contrary, it *firmly resolved* to look seriously and honestly at the ways in which it was communicating—or not really communicating in any meaningful way—with the community, and vowed to introduce significant changes to its practices. Among the key things it did to address the issue:

- It formed a community/school based committee with a good representation of stakeholders, including teachers, administrators, businesspeople, and so on. Rather than treat the group as a mere public relations shell game, it held hands-on meetings exploring the programs the district was trying to implement, being candid about both their strengths and weaknesses, and asking for serious input on how to improve and how best to get the message about what the district was doing out to the rest of the population.
- It understood that pictures actually *are* worth much more than words in most cases, so it communicated its programs and results by graphs and charts, rather than essays filled with esoteric descriptions fit only for the state and federal bureaucracy. The charts and graphs visually and vividly told clear stories. Where were tax dollars being used? How were individual schools and grade levels doing on Adequate Yearly Progress? What did absenteeism or test scores or graduation rates look like over the last three years?
- It redesigned its communication pieces to the public, particularly newsletters that highlighted the partnerships it was forming with members of the community, especially businesses and political decision makers. It pictorially underscored the district's mission, vision, values, and goals in all of its other communications with ma-

jor influential members, and found ways to give out awards to those who put the time and effort in to help the district.
- Administrators and teachers became more visible in the community, seeking out service clubs and other organizations to join and work with. Students were engaged to help out with charity drives for good causes by being given recognition for their community service. In short, the school district *redefined and exhibited itself* as a vital part of the community, not an enterprise apart and opposed to it.

All right, so what happened? It took time, but more and more supporters and even new champions of the school district began to come forward. Key members of the political, business, and religious communities started seeing themselves as partners in the educational goals of the district, and a clear and solid sense of pride became more palpable. Budgets were supported, complaints were diminished considerably, and the district realized it now had a powerful resource of citizens in its corner.

Speaking of budget issues, these are particularly important ones to get the community not only to fully understand, but to enthusiastically support. A proposed budget, after all, is not merely an abstract list of financial ideas, but a blueprint for where and how the money is going to be spent, namely, what the educational values and priorities actually are for the district. Budgets are examples of the value-laden goals that the enterprise seeks to achieve to keep its mission alive and its vision magnetic.

Districts that succeed in getting their budgets approved and supported are exactly the ones that spend time educating the key community members—parents, business groups, political people—to demonstrate the *connection* between the funds being sought and the educational outcomes connected to them. Those districts do this not by passive or mass market approaches, but by targeting citizens with a strong and practical message, and by using personal techniques such as special meetings, neighborhood coffees, fielding tables at town events, asking for time at Rotary and Lions Club lunches, and so on.

There is a crucial mindset question here that we believe is extremely important, one that is almost never flatly addressed and that we have concluded is at the root of so many of the other barriers to genuine educational excellence. It is this: many of the problems and negative energy that schools attribute to their communities actually begin with those schools conceiving of the citizens in their town or city as forces to be ignored, or gotten around, or manipulated, rather than as *essential partners* who must be worked with, partners who can support the mission, vision, values, and goals of the district and help schools do a better job of achieving genuine success.

Yes, there will be naysayers in every community, but the parents and other citizens who understand that an effective and thriving school district can only benefit the political, economic, social, and cultural future of the population can serve as very strong collaborators. We must, however, sincerely decide to treat them that way. The most successful districts are the ones that not only understand this, but work to make sure it forms part of their constant consciousness. The educational leaders of these districts are authentic leaders, committed to treating not only school personnel with the respect they are morally due, but all members and other stakeholders in the same way.

In our next chapter we'll take a look at how one school not only brought the community over to its side as a supporter, but actually got the community's help in improving academic quality and student life.

Fourth Excuse: "Change is something our teachers by nature resist."

Reply: "Have you thought about why anyone has difficulty embracing change? Or aren't you willing to change your thinking about change itself?"

This excuse is not just found in the educational community, but seems to be a maxim of many organizations that are looking for ways to justify their lack of success. One doesn't have to be a trained philosopher or psychologist to appreciate the fundamental fact that certain kinds of changes, no matter what business we are in or what form of life we are living, are not things we generally welcome.

When any change or brand-new process or procedure is suddenly and abruptly announced to employees of any organization—especially those who have spent a good deal of time working with the enterprise—the first and normal reaction is, "What's wrong with how we've been doing it up until now?" Not only teachers, but almost everyone *by nature* has some problem with change, not because of who they are but because of what change always involves.

In our work with school leaders and other executives and managers we try to underscore and explain the four stages of change in order to show how introducing change can ideally work for a more constructive outcome:

1. *Resistance*: Any new process, procedure or policy is, of course, unfamiliar; that's the purely logical consequence of its being new. If the change involves a new curriculum, for example, it is going to take some time for even the most professionally seasoned educators to get comfortable with it, even if they see, theoretically at least, the generalized need for it. The resistance is typical and is to be expected.

No doubt, there are levels of resistance, ranging from absolute antagonism to puzzlement. Yet it should be obvious that the key to overcoming resistance of any kind is (a) making the reasons for the change crystal clear, (b) emphasizing that the change has a purpose that is profoundly tied to the mission, vision, values, and goals of the organization and is not being imposed because people are doing a bad job, and (c) seeking sincere input and collaboration on how best to implement the change and how it is working as it is implemented.

Leaders of organizations who announce major changes in how things are going to be done without using this common-sense approach—and, unfortunately, we have seen plenty of them—are actually building complete failure into the process right up front, no matter what else they might imagine they are doing. The rule here quite clearly is this: *the less you treat people like professionals, the more they will resist change.*

2. *Compliance:* This second stage of change is also natural, but, again, there are several levels of it. Even someone who is looking forward to the change will need some time for trial and error until things get to feel comfortable and easier to do. Think about learning a foreign language or how to drive a car, for example. Someone, however, who has not been sold on the value of the change in the first place might have other fish to fry. He or she might engage in what is sometimes called "malicious obedience," the phenomenon of faux compliance that is mechanical, totally lacking in applied judgment, and whose aim is to prove that the change was a terrible mistake in the first place.

These are usually people for whom we have not taken the time or expended the effort to bring on board. They believe they have been disrespected and unappreciated in some way, and even look for hidden motives in the very introduction of the changed system or new policy. Of course, some people might keep playing this phony compliance game no matter what we do. Before one concludes that all is lost here, however, it is generally a very good idea to see what signals were sent, to examine how the change was introduced to see if better and more collaboration, cooperation and teamwork could have been achieved.

3. *Support:* This is, of course, where we want all those affected by and responsible for the implementation of change to be. Support, however, is never a finished stage in the change process, but needs to be continually maintained and energized. Effective school leaders and other executives are constantly seeking collaboration on how new processes can be made to work better for the goals they were meant to achieve, how the changes actually stack up against the core values of the organization, and where more change might be needed as we move forward.

4. *Commitment:* This stage needs little comment, of course. When you're here, you'll know it clearly enough. If you're not, you'll know that, too, unless you make a practice of major league self-delusion.

Our bottom line for this excuse, therefore, should be pretty evident at this juncture. Before any leader offers the resistance to change as a rationale for throwing in the towel, he or she had better *look at how the change was introduced.* Support and commitment for change simply cannot be automatically expected. Treating those who are charged with delivering a new process, product, or system as if their only responsibility is to obey is the authoritarian antithesis of the lessons of authentic leadership, and will certainly multiply the chances of things going wrong.

> Fifth Excuse: "Tenure makes good teaching about as valuable as acne."
>
> Reply: "Are you actually claiming that there are no good teachers who are tenured? Can anyone seriously mean this?"

Over the past few years, tenure has been the target of governors, legislators, business executives, and just about anyone else who can find a bit of space on this rowdy bandwagon. Some of the noise, no doubt, is connected with a wider economic or political agenda, but tenure has always been an acutely controversial subject, since for most people it implies an absolute and irrevocable guarantee of a job, quite irrespective of the performance of the teacher or other jobholder. And, on the assumption that the latter is true, it is seen by detractors as a major disincentive for teachers to do any more than the bare minimum—if that.

Now, in fact, we noted that tenure is *not a job guarantee*, but pointing this out to its many critics doesn't generally do much good. Yes, someone might grant, there are ways to dismiss a tenured teacher who is an abysmal performer or who is wreaking educational havoc in a district, but the legal procedures involved are hugely cumbersome, time and energy consuming, and fraught with many legal traps and other unimagined difficulties. For all practical purposes, any of the superintendents and principals pursuing that route will have their hands pretty well tied, if not handcuffed.

However, before we conclude that we need a Houdini to teach us how to escape from these ironclad administrative bonds, it might be well to remind ourselves of a few of the very important points we made back in an earlier chapter, points we underscored in describing a culture of success and the role that leadership must play in establishing and maintaining it.

High-achieving schools and other organizations, we noted, do not merely have a clear sense of mission, vision, values, and goals but *work on keeping these things uppermost in the daily life of the enterprise.* They do not do this by constantly talking or sending e-mails or memos or uttering slogans, but by making sure they are measuring all of their critically important activities against these standards and monitoring the progress that has to be made. The kinds of questions constantly being asked in these organizations are typically these:

- Is what we are proposing to do going to get us any closer to the organization we are aspiring to become?
- In what specific ways are we actually exemplifying our core values by undertaking this or any other initiative?
- How do we know—not just think—that we are making genuine progress against our critical goals?
- Are our standards and goals challenging enough and are we really passionate about achieving them at all levels of the organization?
- What do we do as a normal practice in our organization to genuinely support all those charged with getting us closer to our vision, and how do we celebrate our achievements?

In this kind of culture, there are very few major surprises. Yes, there will always be things not anticipated; chance will always be part of any organizational life, just as it is in any life. High-achieving organizations, on the other hand, generally have the sense that *they know where they are with respect to the things that really matter.*

If an employee or a particular unit, for example, is having difficulty contributing to the organization's key objectives, this doesn't come as a bombshell to the leadership of the enterprise. It is not discovered long after the damage is done, but early signs of performance problems are seen in the early hours and are clearly evident. This is because in a culture where data-driven appraisals are built into the very fabric of the organization the *right kinds of questions are consistently being asked.* And they are being asked not just by the leadership, but by everyone in the organization. Everyone in the enterprise is constantly monitoring, measuring, and managing progress by data, by fact, by quantifiable appraisals whenever and wherever possible.

Teachers, just like everyone else in the world, do not become nonperformers overnight. And one doesn't have to be a dim-witted romantic to believe that the vast majority of teachers got into the business of education because they wanted to do a good job, to make a difference in the lives of others. The teachers we have met and worked with are people who are motivated by some pretty strong moral imperatives. Consequently, blaming tenure for a teacher's slide into ineffectiveness *is often simply a way of avoiding the truth about what has been going on* in the school or district. The issue might have begun, for example, with the initial recruiting and candidate evaluation process.[4]

Yet even first-rate teachers need support and encouragement, just as the very best ball players or brilliant musicians need assistance from coaches and conductors in order to work at peak performance. Failure in teaching very often comes down to a matter of the lack of an effective coaching policy and treacherous ambiguity about what interventions are appropriate. In one district we have worked with—and we'll examine this district in greater detail later—the administrators were required to do a certain number of observations every week. This was not merely passive listening, but involved discussion in most cases with the teachers about what was observed, including praise for excellent work and constructive suggestions for improving a particular strategy or tactic.

Not only did teachers benefit greatly from this policy of observation and the collaborative communication it engendered, but the principals and other administrators doing the observations were no longer seen as outsiders, as "the management." And they also began to remember what the mission, vision, values, and goals of the district really and concretely meant. In short, administrators were reminded that they were *educational leaders*—and had to constantly act on that realization. The policy was not a program of "Gotcha!" but one in which professional questions were raised and analyzed. A culture of collaboration began to be built with conversation centering on the issues of goals and values.

Of course, teachers who have been at their jobs for many years always run the risk of falling into ruts, of getting stale and relying on the methods and techniques they have always used. This, however, is not necessarily a result of tenure, but happens in many jobs in many industries. Companies that have successfully addressed this problem have, first of all, acknowledged it openly, and secondly, engaged employees in some very serious discussion about what the employees would like to do, what other projects could be taken on in the organization, how the range of responsibilities they have can be enriched.

Jobs, after all, should not be life sentences, and despite the limited range of options for growth and new challenges that might be available in a school, a district or in the wider community, some "out-of-the-box" thinking needs to arise.[5] This will also help open up some good conversation with the community and political and business leaders, something valuable in addressing our other excuses.

Frankly, many of the professional-development programs in school districts we have witnessed over the years should simply be eliminated. Most are one-size fits all in-service days that have become standard lampoons. Few of them, if any, are put together and delivered in accordance with what the professionals in the district actually need. And, since no one has *actually asked them about what they need*, they are invariably the kinds of programs that deserve to be parodied.

"The fault," Cassius says in *Julius Caesar*, "lies not in our stars, but in ourselves." Although the context of this quote is quite different than our present one, it might be well to remember it when we label tenure the cause of performance failure. Authentic leadership, we said, doesn't look for excuses, no matter how tempting it might be to grab hold of the juicy-looking ones hanging from the lower branches.

Sixth Excuse: "School leaders are really terrible models of excellence."

Reply: "Are you sure you've got the right perspective on your own excellence?"

This excuse, we've seen, is the flip side of the one used by some administrators to blame teachers for low performance, whether the culprit is tenure or resistance to change in general. In other words, it is what one might overhear members of the teaching staff say about the low levels of performance of administrators.

Now, let's be as honest as we can. There is no question that some school districts are plagued by some very poor educational leadership. We've worked with a few tough cases, and denying it would be pointless. Just like teachers, administrators have a wide range of stressors on them: boards, regulators, parents, the larger community, teachers themselves, and so on. Just keeping up with every newly mandated legislative edict and bureaucratic rule-making bulldozing down the pike is bound to take a toll, sometimes in ways that are not obvious.

Yet, two things need to be made clear. First, the majority of the administrators we have worked with, just like the vast majority of teachers, are motivated by high principle, put the education of students above all else and sincerely want to do a good job as leaders. Yes, not all leadership in every school or every district is perfect, but most administrators are trying to do the right kind of job while being faced with more and more pressure by federal, state, and local demands.

Second, the fact that particular administrators are not always performing at peak *does not, of itself, give any teacher an excuse* to throw in the towel and conclude that the quest for excellence is a waste of time. It is one thing if the administrative leadership is actually interfering with the ability of teachers to effectively achieve their purpose, destroying the key values necessary for building a culture of success in the classroom, and making it impossible for a teacher to have any sense of professional self-fulfillment.

It is quite another if all we are really discussing is merely having a less-than-stupendous supervisory environment. In hundreds of business and major nonprofit organizations across the planet, there are many leaders who can stand some very serious improvement. That does not, however, necessarily affect the work of those in the enterprise. A doctor, for example, might be working in a hospital that leaves a great deal to be desired in the CEO's performance, but as a doctor she still needs to work at the very best levels for the sake of her patients.

Like all the excuse-laden justifications we've been examining up to this point, it is simply too easy to blame in some vague and hazy way "the administration" for one's own failures, just as administrators can look for culprits among teachers or the community to hang a noose around as well. Teaching is a very difficult job, and there are more than enough good reasons for things going wrong. Sometimes in frustration we cast our eyes on leadership; this is something done, more often than not, in many other kinds of enterprises, be they businesses or governments.

Yes, one might retort, but what about the worst-case scenario, the nightmare in which there is incompetent and even corrosive control at the top of the district, control that does make it practically impossible to fulfill the mission and goals of real education? Well, sometimes some extremely tough decisions have to be made.

If, on the most objective kind of analysis one can muster and, after getting the best advice possible, there appears to be no way out of the existential fix a teacher is in, leaving the district might be the only realistic option, maybe even the moral option. Heroism makes for good stories, but seldom helps teachers who are trying their best to serve the important needs of the students that society has put in their charge, professionals who are faced with the perverse nightmare of leadership that is destroying genuine education.

Yet even in these extreme situations, some things still need to be tried before taking the next train out of town and concluding that all hope is lost. Beginning the dialogue about the processes—not the people—that seem to be making the educational mission less than effective is a good place to start. Assuming that the intrusive problem is coming from the central office sector, teachers would do best to have that dialogue with their next level of supervision first, namely, the department chair or the master teacher in charge.

At this point the conversation needs to focus on the barriers that seem to be in the way of good teaching and seeking advice and what might be done about them. For example, one might begin the conversation by asking about the level of confidence at work in the autonomy and, therefore, in the capability of the teacher to run his or her own classroom, and what might be done to address the issue clearly. Asking for time to speak to the higher administrative level about the issue in the proper setting, with the agenda clearly established and having a competent moderator in the room, might be the next step in the process.

Unless teachers are clearly living in a genuine House of Horrors— and, yes, we have seen some both in education and elsewhere—it is quite possible that the administrative leadership might not be as aware of how their style of managing the district or the school is affecting educational quality as teachers might believe. There are some risks here, of course, but weighed against the need to get the issue resolved, they might not look so daunting.

Seventh Excuse: "School-board politics will destroy every one of us anyway."

Reply: "Politics serve a purpose, but it is not the only way things get done."

As we mentioned earlier, this excuse by and large hangs its hat on a peg similar to the one naming the community as the villain in the drama. And there can be little doubt that very often school boards reflect both the worst as well as the best views of the community, whether they are elected bodies or appointed ones.

In our experience there are roughly two general complaints that might tend to give some *prima facie* credence to this excuse.

First (the worst case scenario): the board might be politically unprincipled, in the sense that it is driving the individual agendas of some or most members for personal or political gain. This is a corrupt board, and there is probably little that can be done inside the district itself to make things substantially better at the level of policy. Change will have to come from outside, and teachers and administrators should doubtless spend their most productive time working with those political reformers who have some chance of success in rooting out the treachery.

Teachers must still, however, not conclude that what they do in the classroom is no longer of real value, even with a board that has lost its moral compass. Teaching students to achieve *cannot and must not* be put on the shelf while we try to address the distorted aims of those who are ultimately in charge. The board's actions could create an atmosphere that might be frustrating and even disgraceful, but it can never justify giving up the quest for excellence in the classroom.

Second (the more likely state of affairs): one can find a district dealing with a board that is reflecting the particular negative feelings of particular segments of the community. Board members, after all, are in constant contact with the population they represent, and even if the complaints they get are sent over to the administration, the information they receive often raises questions about what's "really" going on in the district. It is very difficult for board members to keep aware of the distinction between their proper role as policy makers and their legitimate interests as agents of the citizenry, a distinction sometimes complicated by the fact that several of them might be parents of children in the district as well.

This latter case is the one that cannot be used as an excuse for administrators giving up the ghost to work for high achievement in a school district, just as we saw that teachers would be ill-advised to drop high standards of performance on the grounds that the leadership was not all it should be. What it calls for from the superintendents and their cabinets, as well as solid support from all levels of the district, including teachers, is a *continuous and data-based campaign of communication with the board of education*, a focused and professionally executed campaign that demonstrates—just as it does with the community—what is, in fact, "really" going on.

The campaign is not a one-shot affair, but is part of the warp and woof of how the board gets its information. Among the key points of the communication:

- What is the vision for the district?
- How is this vision connected to our critical mission?
- What goals are being pursued throughout the district?
- What are the key measures being used to track these goals?
- How do we intervene if necessary to redirect resources toward the achievement of these goals?

Here again, it is important that status reports on these and other issues, including budgets, be made as clear and as visually demonstrated as possible, including trends over time periods. Giving board members crammed lists of endless financial and other numbers alone will seldom work as valuable communication tools. Boards that *get clear, relevant, and memorable information of this kind on a regular basis* will get used to hearing about the right kinds of things, the things that really matter for evaluating the progress of the district. Their questions about the district will tend to be more strategic than operational.

In addition, the members will start to become more aware that their policy role is the right one, since matters of educational practice are in good hands and under control. A key idea we stress in our Academy sessions is the critical importance of the main educational leader in a district working collaboratively and professionally with the board president or chairperson. At the very least it involves sharing agenda items before any full board or committee meetings, and agreeing on a process for keeping the discussion focused on the relevant things while still encouraging meaningful discussion.

It is worthwhile to keep reminding ourselves that businesses and other nonprofits also report to boards of directors, just like school districts do. Boards are not only facts of life in any organization of significant size and complexity, but handled correctly can be strong allies in building a culture of excellence and an atmosphere where success is the rule, not the exception. The best kind of thinking for school leaders is not to jump into the Blame Game with their boards, but to start examining how they can markedly improve their own role in the real game of educational high achievement.

A FEW MORE POINTS ABOUT ELIMINATING EXCUSES

The next chapter will go into much more detail about the tools we have been discussing here, with particular emphasis on systems thinking. These excuses have causes, and these kinds of causes, even for similarly occurring effects in any school or school district, have to be specifically uncovered and addressed. Plans must then be deployed to not only eliminate the cause of the problem but standardize the solution so that we reduce the likelihood of it happening again.

Our last chapter will more directly address some of the things that could still stand in the way of high achievement. We call them "potholes" not to minimize them but to point out how they can be quite serious, just as some potholes can sometimes shatter the most important systems in a motor vehicle. We will spend a good bit of time discussing them for the very reason that their importance cannot be played down.

The tools and approaches we have outlined above, however, are not to be thought of a "soft-headed" or some form of simple folk wisdom. They are the tried and true means by which the best-run organizations with committed leaders, whether schools or hospitals, work to maintain a culture of excellence and high achievement. They are not easy and will not magically appear out of the wings. Excellence in educational leadership never happens by sleight of hand.

IDEAS FOR FURTHER CONSIDERATION

In our second chapter we deployed for you the Eight Lessons of Authentic Leadership.

Take a few minutes to look them over again. Which of those concepts do you believe are essential for effectively using the tools we explained to address each excuse in this chapter? In other words, how do you think those leadership skills line up against the specific resources we claimed are needed to address the problem?

For example, the Fourth Excuse that the faculty and staff are invincibly resistant to any meaningful change requires the leadership skill to find ways to make followers into leaders and to maximize as much freedom and innovation as possible in the school or district. What are some ways of doing this? The Sixth Excuse, that administrators are looked on by teachers and staff as poor models of excellence, might require a serious look by the educational leadership about how they actually view the power they have, if they are involved in the self-deception of confusing titles with leadership, or if the values they are demonstrating in their everyday practice are questionable.

Take some time to think about other excuses and their relationship with the Lessons of Authentic Leadership. All of the tools we have talked about and the ones still to be analyzed will require consistently practiced and effective leadership in order to become integrated into the culture of a school seeking to attain excellence.

NOTES

1. Like the joke, this is not that funny. We've heard versions of this excuse in more than one organization we have worked with.

2. Although not specifically geared to elementary and high-school students, the essay "Motivating Students" by the University of Wisconsin's Whitewater School of Graduate studies has some solid advice about engaging students in the learning process in a substantive, nonartificial way. The site is at: www.uww.edu/learn/motivating students.

3. We warned you that we would keep doing this reiterating thing, didn't we?

4. From the perspective of many human resource professionals we have worked with, this is a prevalent weakness in many of even the best organizations. A worthwhile guide on these issues in Richard Luecke's *Hiring and Keeping the Best People* (Boston: Harvard Business School Press, 2003).

5. Pasi Sahlberg's book, *Finnish Lessons: What Can the World Learn from Educational Change in Finland?* (New York: Teachers College Press, 2011) shows definitively that the Finns regard teaching and teacher education to be as important as the training and value assigned to professions like medicine or law. Teachers are treated as professionals, given freedom to use their own teaching methods, given lots of time and space daily to collaborate with other teachers and staff, and stress problem solving and critical thinking with their students. Finnish educators, by the way, can never be accused of "teaching to the test" since Finland does not use standardized tests. Yet students consistently perform at the top levels of international tests.

FIVE

Can These Things Work in Any School? Even Mine? You're Kidding!

Anyone who has begun to think places some part of the world in jeopardy.
—John Dewey

First things first. Well, how about first things at least one more time. Because before we roll up our sleeves and get into thick of the tools we are going to unpack for you, let's briefly revisit two earlier ideas that are going to be vital for us to keep in mind, namely, change and leadership.

Change—especially major change—we have noted more than once in earlier comments is never easy, so as we move into the next, and more

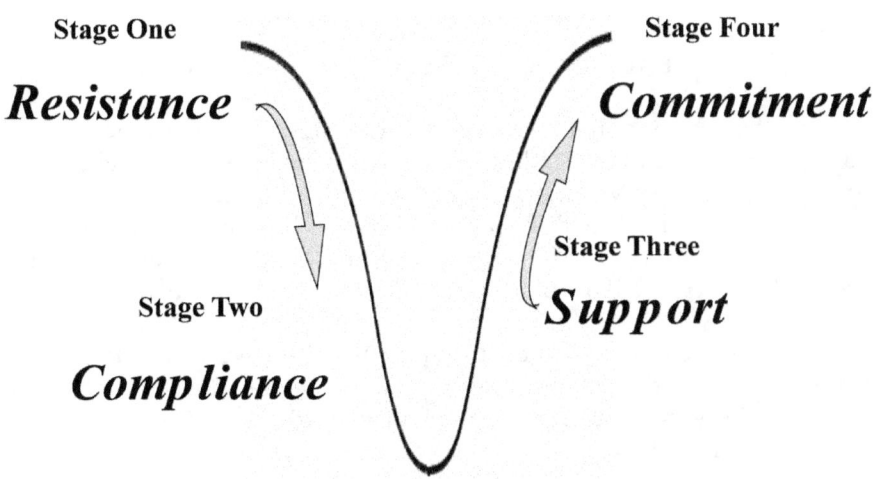

Figure 5.1.

specific tools that are necessary to get closer to high-achievement, it might be valuable to recall the four stages of change we discussed earlier. This chart illustrates them more graphically for us.

Note that these are *stages*, not instantaneous periods of automatic enlightenment. Introducing and using these tools will take time, both for those who do the introducing and for those who need to get fully on board with them. That is also why we keep talking about (1) the kinds of excuses that can lead to frustration, inaction, and eventual surrender to mediocrity in a school or school system, and (2) the critical tools one must have for addressing these excuses.

Tools, however, no matter how first-rate and well made, won't work by themselves. People have to know how to use them, have to be convinced of their value, and have to be supported by an organizational structure and an environment that encourages their focused, consistent use. In short, the prerequisite is a culture that will not settle for anything less than (at least) seriously trying to apply the new methodology. Our experience consistently tells us that when case-hardened resistance to change is the first thing we encounter in any organization, this essential transformation is extraordinarily difficult.

So, if nothing good ever happens in one fell swoop, then anyone who believes that an organizational culture can be turned around by simply announcing a new direction or organizational strategy is blissfully ignoring some durable, relevant facts about human nature, the most important one of which is that change is always intimidating. Two indispensable things are required for even the beginnings of success: authentic leadership and the relentless dedication to a realistic model that can guide all stakeholders to higher achievement using the tools we have begun to discuss.

LEADERSHIP UNDERSCORED (AGAIN)

We have been saying that it is safer, and we think smarter, to risk repeating ourselves instead of treading too lightly on our most important ideas. And so we need to give renewed emphasis to the key point that authentic and effective leadership is *absolutely essential* to building a culture of excellence in all parts of the school building and system. No tool works by itself. When? How? For what purpose? Under what particular circumstances?

These are the critical and controlling questions that have to be consistently asked if successful outcomes are going to materialize. The practices of authentic leadership are essential to execution, and will also help greatly in our next chapter when we discuss ways of avoiding the "potholes" that our journey to high achievement is bound to encounter.

Let's remember, however, some of the key things that successful leaders in any organization consistently and constantly practice—whether they are schools, small businesses, or multinational corporations: They

- communicate a strong, clear, *actionable vision* throughout the organization, a vision that serves as the framework in terms of which all major decisions made need to be evaluated;
- adopt and encourage throughout the organization a *questioning spirit*, not accepting the status quo as dogma and always seeking for meaningful ways to improve and for measures to assess these improvements;
- lead with clear *moral character*, for they are people who are genuinely dedicated to the excellence of the organization and whose word and work can always be trusted;
- promote *freedom and innovation* throughout the enterprise, constantly signaling their readiness to listen to others and to value their perspective—in short, they treat everyone in the organization as a contributor with something important to say;
- avoid confusing their leadership with power, authority or titles; by *avoiding power trips* and authority traps they follow the motto of the Chinese thinker Lao Tzu: "To lead one must follow."

The best tools and models and brilliantly drawn graphs and charts will not and cannot, therefore, do anything *by themselves* to turn things around in any organization that is falling short of high-achievement. Organizational life of any kind is always a thoroughly human life, no matter what any simplistic manuals about management might tell us. And education is that thoroughly human life written in even larger and bolder colors. It is never the manipulation of inanimate objects or abstract policies. We must not forget this as we go forward.

THE MODEL: PLAN-DO-CHECK-ACT

We've said that the most successful organizations are without doubt the ones characterized by a clear focus on the direction in which they are heading and by an unambiguous commitment to a model that will get them there.

The model might look quite simple, and, in fact, we have used the essential elements of it earlier: *Plan-Do-Check-Act*. The paradigm has been around for nearly a century and was developed in the 1920s by Walter A. Shewhart, a pioneer in the application of statistical methods to mass production. Its simplicity, however, conceals a scheme of considerable power, for it lies at the very heart of the commitment to quality.

Businesses are not the only ones that have adopted some version of the model, but many schools have also begun to embrace it, especially as

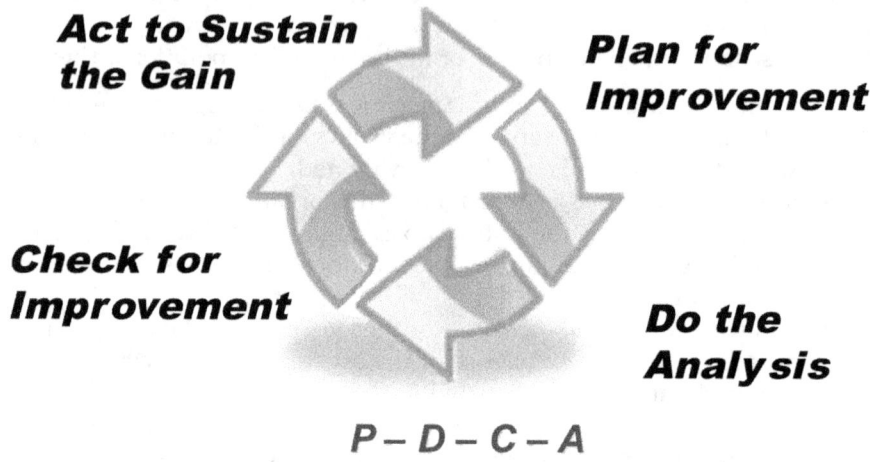

Figure 5.2.

the leaders in those schools and districts make more and more meaningful commitments to decision making that is data-driven. [1]

SYSTEMS THINKING AND LEADERSHIP

The Shewhart model is our first and most basic concept in systems thinking. In many respects, throughout our lives we often, but mostly nonreflectively, rely on it.

Take the simple case of deciding to take a long vacation trip by car. Your first move, of course, is to *PLAN* the journey. What roads should I take? Is the vehicle in safe condition? What is the ultimate destination? About how long will it take to get there? What stops will we make along the way? Your next move is *DO*. So you get started on the trip driving carefully and safely. Along the way, of course, the journey will often require that you *CHECK* on how things are going. Should you stop for more gasoline? A coffee break?

This step is especially important if things are not shaping up as you hoped or predicted. A highway you were planning on using is shut down because of a major emergency. You're getting a low-oil-pressure warning on your dash board. Whatever the case, the original plan will have to be adjusted and you will have to *ACT*. And, as you can quickly see, you are right back into starting the cycle again, this time with revised planning.

Notice also that many of the pursuits in our lives begin with the doing part of the cycle. That is, we find ourselves caught up in routines and procedures that we have used often, that we are comfortable with, and that we come to think of as "normal" and "natural" but have suddenly become problematic. Hence the built-in reluctance we have to change our approach, unless some unexpected failure happens. A classic case is the person feeling ill, going to the doctor (*Check*) and being told by the doctor that he or she has to change diets (*Act*) or serious health consequences are going to occur. So, of course, a new *Plan* has to be put in place and that, too, has to be regularly checked on (and acted on accordingly) to be sure we are on course to get the right outcome.

We promised in previous pages that we would tighten up and make more rigorous our description of the tools needed to beat back the excuses that persist in keeping schools from getting closer to high-achievement. And we will begin that process now by revisiting those seven excuses and applying the techniques of systems thinking to them. So let's talk for a bit about what we mean by systems thinking. As you will see as we put the tools to use in the following discussions, the heart of systems thinking can be captured by these key points.

Systems thinking, as we'll use it in an educational setting:[2]

- begins with a thorough and fact-based description of the high-priority issues and problems that must be addressed if measurable progress is to be made in a district or school;
- requires, therefore, fully understanding what actually counts as progress and how it is to be measured;
- demands an uncompromising and solid analysis of which educational and other processes effectively work and which do not and why; and
- necessitates continual feedback on and control of the key factors that affect the critical outcomes that the school or school district is seeking to achieve.

It should go without saying—although it still seems worth saying more than just once—that in our Academy experience the hallmark of the systems approach to addressing any important issue is *disciplined, consciously focused and unbiased* analysis. This is never easy, even for the most recalcitrant policy wonks. Since our beliefs are part and parcel of the concept we have of our identity, of who we are as persons, they are extremely difficult to hold up for objective and unprejudiced inspection and analysis. We have to keep striving for that objectivity, however, because letting our guard down on this score usually risks failure.

Leadership and systems thinking are the partners that form the critical architecture of the *Journey to High Achieving Schools* ™, a model we created and that has helped transform typical classroom instructional practices into performance management systems aimed at achieving excellence. We'll say more about the model later. Now, as promised, let's begin to revisit the excuses and apply some tools with a slightly different but even more powerful focus.

The acronym we need you to first think about is *"IDEAS"* The letters stand for the following:

"I" Identify the problem you are trying to address
"D" Determine the root cause of the problem
"E" Explore possible solutions that could eliminate or reduce the problem
"A" Assess the results of deploying those solutions
"S" Standardize the improvements that have been made

We have already, of course, seen and generally addressed the importance of the first letter—the problem—when we asked what specifically one might possibly mean by Excuse Number One, namely, that the rest of the world could not possibly understand the tough and unmanageable problems educators have. We now want you to see that problem identification and analysis are part of a larger and systematic approach to eliminating the excuse-riddled mindset. (If it looks like we are treading on ground we might have already strolled over with you, trust us and enjoy the walk.)

THE EXCUSES REEXAMINED: THE POWER OF *IDEAS*

EXCUSE NUMBER ONE: You Just Don't Get Our Problem

Figure 5.3.

REPLY: Trust me, I get it!

TOOL NEEDED: A process to develop problem statements that are truly actionable.

We mentioned before that this can be one of the most difficult and most critical excuses to overcome, simply because many people tend to believe they have the solution before they have clearly defined what the problem is. This is especially the case if the problem is stated in such a vague and ambiguous way that almost anything seems captured by it. Just as we saw in our first brush with our first excuse, most organizations also tend to take the attitude that unless you have walked in my shoes you can't possibly understand what my problem is and therefore any suggested strategy from an "outsider" just will not work.

Educational organizations demonstrate this belief quite consistently as we have witnessed while working with them both in our Academy sessions and in other settings in which we have tried to help them use this first quality tool. At the root of it might be, among other things, the seemingly deeply ingrained view that (a) to be an effective teacher you must figure out how to quickly and successfully solve your own problems, and (b) to serve as an effective administrator you have to be the heroic and courageous firefighter who slides down the firehouse pole and responds quickly, whatever the nature of the problem and however it's presented.

These two emotional viewpoints can lead to something similar to playing the carnival game called "Whack-A-Mole." The little devils keep relentlessly and annoyingly popping up no matter how many you smack down. The whole point of the game for most of us appears to be making sure we fail, for no matter how fast and accurate you are at knocking them down, they will just keep returning.

This is exactly what happens when organizations or individuals do not take the time to carefully and clearly identify the problem. It is even worse, however, because the carnival game keeps the same infuriating pace. In a school setting what usually occurs is that the quick remedies that are used do not get to the real cause. So the problem keeps recurring, of course. Perhaps what is even more damaging is that leaders and others begin to conclude that it's just not a solvable problem, one of those "things we'll just have to live with."

But a day might dawn when it can't be "lived with" anymore, when it explodes into something not only much more damaging, but impossible to handle with the usual routine response. The key to avoiding this frustration and the disasters that can follow in its wake is to gain mastery of this first tool of *IDEAS*.

We mentioned *SMOG* in passing when we looked at the first excuse in the last chapter. Let's now look at it in more detail. The idea behind

"Identifying the Problem" is this: *the only way anyone can do anything about a problem is to make sure they fully understand it*. SMOG, with the small letter "p" added on as we'll note, helps us get this done. The statement of the problem must:

- (S) Be *specific* enough to describe the problem and its effects so it is not confused with something else,
- (M) Show a clear means of *measuring* the scope of the problem, so that there is a way of indicating if and when data-based progress can be made on it,
- (O) Be *objectively stated*, so that the cause of the problem is not assumed in the problem's description,
- (G) Point out *the gap* between the present situation and what would count as future progress on it, and
- (p) Make some reference to what *pain or distress* is happening (and will likely continue to happen) if the problem is not addressed correctly. This helps us make sure that the problem is an issue worth addressing and not just a passing annoyance.

To help understand how to use the first step of the *IDEAS* process we have listed below two examples of written problem statements followed by a corrected example utilizing the elements of *SMOG* with "p." These are actual examples, by the way, from participants in the Academy for Education Leaders.

Example One:

"The administrations and teachers of Anytown's School District do not have a unified process regarding the examination of data and the de-

SMOGp Reveals

Specific problem: Schools use data differently

Measurable: How these three schools use data

Objective: No solution or cause is mentioned

Gap: Data use differently verses similarly

Pain: Schools operating in isolation, wasted time

Figure 5.4.

velopment of plans based upon data. Currently, the district has several key programs and initiatives to generate data. Due to a lack of a unified process to analyze and implement data plans, each of the three schools uses data in different ways and operates in isolation."

All right, let's apply our *SMOG* test:

- S: The problem is specific, namely, school professionals are using data differently, although what specifically that data is just doesn't seem clear;
- M: Although there is no clear measurement specified, the problem appears to be one that can be measured in some meaningful way;
- O: There is no suggested cause of the problem, although the statement gives the impression that the solution should be connected with seeking a unified process of some kind;
- G: The gap between where we are at present and where we need to be is not clearly defined;
- P: Why this problem is important and needs to be addressed is not mentioned, although one might imagine that it is not a very good thing.

Let's look at another way in which the problem statement might make things clearer:

"Each of the district's three schools uses data differently to analyze and implement key programs and initiatives. As a result, it is difficult to effectively (assess/compare, evaluate strategies or) identify systemic opportunities for improvement. This contributes to schools operating in isolation, wasted time, and/or inefficiencies in the examination of data and the development of plans based upon data."

The difference here should be pretty clear, especially from the *SMOG* point of view. This restatement now allows us to ask the right kinds of meaningful questions and to get moving on some actionable answers. What kind of data are we talking about? How different are the uses to which the data is being put? What effects does the present situation have on students?

Example Two:

"Currently, the Academic Enrichment teachers do not share a common practice for reporting information regarding the students serviced. Without a shared procedure, collecting the information becomes inaccurate and time-consuming."

Our *SMOG* test:

- S: Not overly clear. What kind of information are we talking about? Is this an issue for all enrichment teachers, some teachers, or most teachers?

M: The inaccuracies and time consumption are, of course, measurable in principle, but without more data the gap (G) doesn't hold a lot of promise for getting on with the issue.

O: The cause of the failure for the sharing of a common practice is not assumed, but, again, there seems to be a bias toward the sharing being the solution to the problem. (If we ask, "Why are they not sharing?" the answer surely cannot be "Because they just aren't sharing!")

G: No clear gap is pointed out, although there is a suggestion that it is taking more time than it should.

P: The pain seems to be there, but since the kind of student information we are talking about isn't delineated, we are not sure how big a problem this actually is.

A different rewrite might start this way:

> *"The current process of reporting information regarding students serviced by the Academic Enrichment teachers is time-consuming and often results in inaccurate information."*

Again, this begins to open the door to some useful questions that can be acted upon. What exactly is the current process of reporting? How many students are involved? How often does inaccurate information about the students show up? Regarding the gap issue, are teachers complaining about having to rewrite reports, or have supervisors noticed an increase in the number of inaccuracies? How much more time is being lost or wasted? Ten minutes on average? An hour? The point is that *the need for better data is now clear*. The earlier version of the statement really doesn't give us much of a clue about what to do or where to look or what would count as a good approach to solving the problem.

The great American philosopher, John Dewey, once noted that a problem well stated is already on its way to being solved. But care must be taken not to explicitly state or imply a solution. A teacher who claims that we "have a problem" because we do not have enough computers for students to use in the IT lab is not describing an actionable problem, but is already putting forth a favored solution to what has been previously perceived as some kind of problem.

Participants in our *Academy for Education Leaders* sometimes ask us why we spend so much time on problem identification and problem statements, especially time trying to avoid building into the problem description the subtle implication of the cause. The reason is that if this first step in the *I.D.E.A.S.* process goes awry, invariably *so will everything else that follows it*.[3]

As for surreptitiously allowing an implied cause to creep in, that usually happens unconsciously, and is most likely due to either (a) relying on past experience and the corporate or cultural "wisdom"—something we warned against and that authentic leadership pays particular attention to avoid, or, (b) the fact that educators, like other professionals, feel a need to get to the heart of the matter as soon as they can, so that time is not wasted. But understandable as this might be, special concern has to be given at this critical point of the process.

The problems that educators face may certainly be different in terms of the content they contain and the special knowledge it may take to handle them, but when they are analyzed in terms of the specific requirements for actionable process, they are structurally not unlike the major problems faced by many other organizations, whether businesses or nonprofits. And that is why systems thinking and solid, authentic leadership can successfully address both kinds.

EXCUSE NUMBER TWO: Students just aren't interested in learning.

REPLY: What demonstrated facts justify this claim? Have you searched for the cause?

TOOL NEEDED: Clarify the claim. Then, brainstorm to determine the root cause.

In our first review of this excuse, we pointed out the temptation to jump to any cause available to back the legitimacy of the claim—parents, teachers, the Internet, games, and so on. You might remember that that one of the major points we were arguing for was the need for *real data* in this excuse, data that is seldom forthcoming when these kinds of sweeping claims are made. The *I.D.E.A.S.* process *insists that data is absolutely essential here.* In fact, as we've already seen in our discussion of problem statements, without data we truly do not know what we are talking about, and much of what we believe to be true is staggeringly devoid of genuine evidence.

Let's start by considering a point that might seem obvious: If learning is a natural process like eating, drinking, walking, and talking, then it should clearly follow that cognitive learning is a natural process as well. The belief that some children absolutely cannot learn is a view that we do not subscribe to, nor is it the view of any serious educator. Similar to the way children get excited about learning sports, dance, or games, the excitement that engenders reading and writing usually occurs because the child is trying to emulate or please a parent or some other adult figure.

Research tells us that the sooner we start children in preschool or any other early educational environment, the child's ability to learn and retain knowledge will definitely be enhanced. And this, of course, makes success in the formal schooling that follows all the more likely.[4] Psychologists also tell us that all children are quite unique in the interests and abilities they bring to the formal learning process.

Even in these early preschool experiences we already begin to observe that some children are not fitting into the traditional classroom model. Getting to know such children, understanding how they learn, discovering their interests and motivators, and how they demonstrate their values and the beliefs connected with them are critical to having the new students stay interested in the formal learning process.

Creating individual educational plans for every child used to be an extremely cumbersome and time-consuming process, but with today's technology it is beginning to become a much more achievable reality. Of course, not all school districts have this technology, not to mention the special staff to keep it current. Yet, what is possible is to have all students learn about themselves.

We are not suggesting psychoanalytic probing, but an approach that helps students understand the ways in which they learn new things, how to identify the values that form the key drivers of their relationships with others and how they see the importance of those relationships. This line of attack can help students to begin to understand why they do what they do—the why and the how of it. And this, quite logically, leads to students getting a better *sense of ownership for their learning* and becoming more accountable for both their successes and opportunities for improvement.

In some of the districts we have consulted with, we have guided the staff and their students in using personality assessments and value ranking to help them learn how they energize, how they gather information, how they make decisions, and how they develop the key elements of a life style. This information is an excellent window for staff and students to gain priceless knowledge of their teaching and learning styles and how they connect with each other. We then group this information into the four temperaments that come from standard personality assessments. The temperaments can, of course, conflict as well as match.[5]

We also run this exercise with the participants in our Academy for Education Leaders to get them to understand how to work more productively with other administrators, parents, community leaders and teachers. These kinds of discoveries are uniformly enlightening experiences for all, and feedback on their value are common.

The *IDEAS* process started with a very specific and actionable statement of what the current situation is that we want to improve. If the statement was not actionable, we kept stressing, then determining the true cause for the problem has almost no real chance. The murkier the problem description, the increased probability that the wrong source for it will be concluded.

The "D" in *IDEAS* stands for determining the root cause, not anything that we might *think* is at the root of the problem. And that means solid data has to be collected using the kinds of questions that will only be satisfied by objective analysis, data that is demonstrably relevant to the issue at hand. This collection of relevant data can often turn out to be quite surprising to our initial assumptions, even to experts with long experience who live by objective facts. In one of the Sherlock Holmes stories, for example—*The Crooked Man*—the great detective confesses this revelation to his colleague:

> *"You know my methods, Watson. There was not one of them that I did not apply to the inquiry. And it ended by my discovering traces, but very different ones from those which I had expected."*

The excuse, therefore, that "students just aren't interested in learning" immediately cries out for facts to justify the claim. And if we have those facts in hand, the next question surely must be, "*Why does this occur*? Or are you simply claiming that this phenomenon hasn't any cause?" Would we settle for that kind of logic from an engineer who tells us there is no cause for a bridge collapse? Or from a physician when we have asked for the cause of some painful set of symptoms?

If one truly wishes to determine *why* students appear not interested in learning, one has to start collecting key data very early in the formal schooling process so that a systematic pursuit of the cause can get off the ground.

Some relevant data to collect might be:

- School attendance
- School participation
- Quality of work
- Social interactions
- Emotional maturity
- Data on nutrition, physical status, etc.

Some information on the trends of this data over time is also helpful, since it can offer some clues about the relationship of the data with other events. And that is why, as we've said, that collecting this data as well as monitoring the participation and behavior of the parent or guardian will often present instructive evidence both for framing the "I" in *IDEAS* more coherently—namely a more useful identification of the problem being posed ("Why students aren't interested in learning")—but can lead to the next important step in the Problem-Solving Process: "D" for Determine the Root Cause. This next step is, as we'll see, one of the most critical in systems thinking. Before we describe it, we will need to make a few more points about the overall context for *IDEAS*.

BRAINSTORMING AND ROOT CAUSES

Here is a maxim we simply cannot stress enough: the *IDEAS* process is a *collaborative process*, and is not one that can be successfully accomplished in isolation from one's colleagues. All of the tools we have been and will be discussing are not offered as opportunities for a monologue carried on in seclusion, and have almost no chance of being effective in such a monastic setting.

Good problem statements, for example, normally result from the give-and-take that professionals bring to the table. The discussion and exchange of viewpoints not only minimizes the chance that one person's assumptions will drive the outcome down a narrow path, but also offers a much higher probability of breaking through the bonds of the "normal" way of doing business.

This also applies to the collection of facts and data to better analyze any issue, especially with a view toward finding the root cause. The sorts of data we bring forward, for example, are usually determined by the framework we think will give us the best chance of making progress on the problem; philosophers call this "abduction" or "inference to the best explanation." When different people in the dialogue bring diverse views on what data is relevant and what might be immaterial, we allow for a much wider view of the terrain.

Brainstorming techniques, as most of us know, are nothing new, and are lately being studied much more often and in a great deal of depth, although not always so unfortunately, by academic psychologists. Particularly when brainstorming for the cause of a problem, among the fundamental points that users of the method must keep constantly in mind are:

a. avoid evaluation of the ideas as they are being collected and displayed—there are no "bad" ideas at the brainstorming stage;
b. make sure the atmosphere is collegial and comfortable—this is not boot camp and there are no penalties for running out of ideas;
c. involve the right people—the people who know the actual situation or problem that needs to be addressed;
d. do not try to solve the problem—the aim is to come up with potential causes for it that will need to be handled later on; and
e. no one in the room outranks anyone else—which is why the CEO or other supervisory types should generally not lead the process of collecting and categorizing the ideas, since it can be seen as covert evaluation.

In addition, we find it very useful to get the group to use Post-its or something similar to capture the ideas being generated, urge participants to write very brief points on them (say, a noun and a verb), and not let the activity go on for too long a period to avoid fatigue both mental and physical.

Displaying the ideas on a large space in order to categorize them requires that everyone silently put the slips into meaningful groupings. As the slips exhibit connections, headings for the lists should be created and posted. Examples might be: Technology Issues, Curriculum Quality, Counseling Issues, Training. Again, no evaluation allowed.

To find a cause, of course, is always to ask "Why" and to avoid quickly settling for the first answer that comes along. Are the students not getting the right kind of counseling support, we think? Why? Counselors do not have enough hours available for students during the day—why? They each have many additional assignments not related to their primary function? Why? Well . . . You get the idea.

There is nothing automatic or even foolproof about determining the root cause. That's why *CHECK* is a crucial part of *P-D-C-A*. The process is a combination of logic, experience, creative thought and, sometimes, a kind of indefinable "enlightenment." Discussion and conceptual testing often has to occur—for example, "Why is this happening only in School A and not School B?" or "Why did this problem begin only last year and not the year before?" or "If C is the root cause of the problem, why does it still keep occurring after we got rid of it?" Again, that is why the more carefully delineated the problem statement is, the better your chance at finding the root cause. Murkiness and muddiness is the enemy of progress here, just as it is in all of systems thinking.

The underlying motto of brainstorming is "No one of us is smarter than all of us." In several of the organizations we have worked with, we are sometimes amazed to discover that the brainstorming process is either seldom used or/and not taken seriously when it is.

Quite aside from the value the method offers for finding causes and recommending courses of action to address important issues, using the technique sends an extremely important signal to the employees of any organization *that they matter*, that the organization needs their ideas, and that they are not mere mindless cogs in the impersonal mechanism of the institution. The tools of systems thinking gain as well from this teamwork and cooperation; in fact, collaboration is not just a nice idea but is essential for them to be effective. It is a small wonder that authentic leadership also gains from this kind of teamwork.[6]

EXCUSE NUMBER THREE: Our Community Doesn't Support Us.

REPLY: Have you ever given it the chance?

TOOLS NEEDED: Collaborate, identify, find causes and work toward solutions.

If teamwork and collaboration are crucial to the culture of any organization, a little thought will easily establish that schools gain from working with those who are outside of the formal organization as well. As we've argued, communities usually support their local school, especially when that school genuinely looks upon its community as a key stakeholder in the educational process.

We are not talking about lip service and platitudes regarding the town, city, or village in which the school district is located. Often these banalities are simply ways of keeping "outsiders" at their comfortable distance. At the bottom are the same reasons that lurk behind Excuse Number One, namely, that anyone who is not on the "inside" could not possibly understand what educators are going through—and, of course, it follows that they could not possibly help.

This is a major mistake. Communities are made up of parents, businesses, involved citizens, political officials, and many others who understand that good schools are important to the life of the city, town, or village in which they exist. The members of the community, however, will not see themselves as key stakeholders and supporters of the schools unless they are invited in to play a genuine role and are not treated as window dressing. The board of education, the superintendent and central administration, and school leadership have to involve them in strategic planning, focus groups, and in the review of key performance and operational data.

Here's an example from our experience:

A blue-collar high school had developed the reputation of being nowhere even near a high-performing academic institution. The public perception was, in addition, that students were given to constant fighting and other kinds of violence to solve routine disagreements, often over trivial matters. Clearly, with this kind of perceived status, the people in the community were not exactly lining up to sing the school's praises.

To change this perception and engage the community as a true supporter, the school leaders, with backing from the superintendent and board of education, first made a significant and serious review of the mission, vision, values, and goals of the school and involved the entire school community.

Next, a school advisory committee was developed consisting of staff, students, parents, central administrators, local police, and business and civic group members. The committee met three times during the school year over a period of four years. The first meeting would take place in early September once the school had completed the opening adjustments to the master schedule; the second meeting would be held close to the mid-point of the school year; the third meeting would be held usually during the last full month before the school year ended.

Initially the committee worked with the school leadership assisting with "I" in *IDEAS*, identifying the specific problem causing the negative perceptions of the school. Then the committee was divided into groups charged with "D," namely, determining the root cause of the problem. With the root cause(s) of the problem identified the committee then worked on "E," exploring possible solutions to the root cause(s).

This initial work was best done during the summer break to allow enough time for the members to reach out to their own constituents and work together to do a more thorough job of analysis. When the committee held the September session, the members brought back the information it gathered during the summer break and reviewed again the school's mission, vision, values, and goals. With the review completed the committee began the process of brainstorming possible solutions to eliminate the identified root cause(s).

Once all the possible solutions are identified through the brainstorming process and placed on flip chart paper and posted for all to see the next step is to reduce all these potential solutions down to the critical few. The real key to this process—just like the key to all effective collaboration—is *keeping all committee members engaged* and not allow the overpowering by any strong personalities. The specific tools that are used to do this are called Nominal Group Technique (NGT) and "Solution Matrices."

NOMINAL GROUP TECHNIQUE AND SOLUTION MATRICES

NGT, like many of the tools in *IDEAS*, is used to minimize lengthy unproductive discussion, uncover and make visible divergent viewpoints, and ensure that all group members have contributed and had their voices truly heard. To use NGT you must begin with the list of items—in this case, the possible solutions to address the cause—and the task of the group or team is to narrow the items down to a critical few or even only one. There are three basic steps involved.

Step 1. *Restate, Discuss, and Clarify Items on the Large List*

Start by making sure things are not going to be unwieldy. We recommend working with a manageable list of fewer than ten items, ideally somewhere around five to seven. In our experience, more than ten items can get confusing, so a way needs to be found to whittle it down. Standard techniques such as multivoting or other ways to use prioritizing to get to the most important items are easily available from the Internet, for example, and many other sources.[7] The general idea is to force decisions by making sure the number of items is always larger than the votes any one has available to use. Make sure that there are no duplicate items on the list, and it may be useful to alphabetically label the items to make it easier to identify or discuss them.

Step 2. *Explain the Weighted Voting/Prioritizing Process*

Each member of the team needs to now identify what she or he believes to be the most important or best possible solution that would do the job of addressing the root cause effectively. The team members now rate the items numerically, assigning their top choices a value of five, the next best a four, and so on with their fifth choice getting a value of one. It is all right if items other than the top five do not get a vote.

Step 3. *Talley the Votes*

It should be obvious that the item with the highest score will reflect the consensus of the group. The other ratings also indicate the priorities the team placed on those ideas. In a larger group, it may be easier to break up the process by having smaller groups reach consensus scores first using the same process before soliciting the rankings for each item.

Let's talk about Solutions Matrices. These are project management tools used to define what it will take to implement an idea/solution. In some ways we can think of them as the "real world" version of our potential solutions, since we are now looking into the conditions under which they will actually work. By using a matrix to rate the various methods that could be pursued, a team can rank their opinions regarding:

What possible solutions could eliminate the root cause(s)?
What solutions will have the greatest impact on the problem?
What solutions are the most cost-effective?
What solutions can be feasibly implemented?

Solutions Matrices provide a visual instrument to align each root cause with a potential solution and to identify how each potential solution will be implemented.

Now, back to our School Advisory Committee. Let's find out what happened.

The principal aim of their second meeting, usually held mid-school year, was to check progress on the solutions they had agreed upon, and to and to make any changes suggested by the data and other facts they were measuring.[8]

The committee's third meeting was geared toward making the final analysis of the data and metrics—*how things are actually working*—and recommending keeping and standardizing the solutions that showed actual evidence of eliminating the root cause(s). An implementation plan was devised to introduce throughout the entire school, and this process required the development of a detailed action plan.

So how did this all work out in the end? Although there was clearly no quick fix involved—there seldom is in complex issues of this kind—

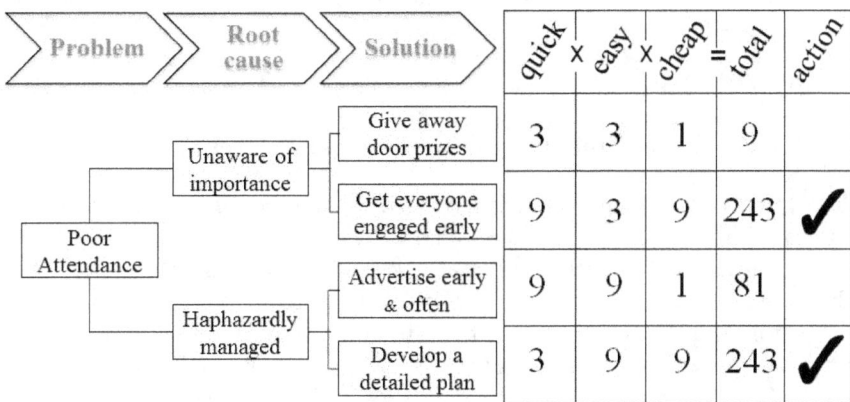

Figure 5.5. A Typical Solutions Matrix

through a lot of hard creative work by the larger community, the school changed the perceptions of its poor academic image and aggressive student behavior. However—and much more importantly—since the perceptions were not imaginary, using this process actually and significantly improved the school's academic quality and achievement and virtually eliminated violence as the means students resorted to for solving problems.

There is an extremely valuable lesson here. Not blaming, but actually *engaging* the community—getting to know it, using its strengths and expertise, appealing to its genuine desire to help—these are the first crucial things to getting rid of this excuse that is too often lodged in the mind set of professional educators. The community is not a resource that you have to deal with, but can be one that you must deal with, if your school is to gain a leg up on high achievement.

What is absolutely essential as well, however, is having *a proven process by which measurable, real improvement can be made.* Simply putting people in a room with no structure for addressing the issues that matter to your school's or district's future will get you nowhere, and get you there faster than you thought possible. This is one reason why many people would rather tame a lion than attend a committee meeting. Paradoxically, despite the speed with which the effort can crash and burn, much time will have been wasted in the attempt.

Good people and good intentions need good systems for getting good things done.

EXCUSE NUMBER FOUR: Change is something our teachers by nature resist.

REPLY: So does everyone else.

TOOL NEEDED: Training and support in key process thinking.

We argued earlier that the suspicious view we take when change of any kind faces us is not peculiar to teachers. Human nature as a rule tends to resist change. Yet people and many kinds of organizations and even schools have made and continue to make significant changes.

Schools that have moved in the direction of high achievement have not done this by accident, however. Meaningful change is generally the result of (a) seriously engaging educators in the process that will direct the change, (b) collecting key data and analyzing that data in visible ways by illustrating it through charts and graphs, and (c) skilled leaders who have been trained in systems analysis, process identification, and careful management.

Ready for another acronym? (Of course you are!) Let us introduce *SIPOC*.

SIPOC stands for:

Suppliers Inputs Processes Outputs Customers

The power of this model is that it helps to clarify and distinguish the process measures that can assist teams in identifying and implementing strategies to achieve excellent teaching. It is based on the work of Edward Deming, known as "The Father of Quality."

Take a noneducational example first to get a better handle on it.

You decide to go into the restaurant business and open up a pizza shop. Here are your questions:

1. Who do I need to work with to get the business up and running?
2. What materials, information, regulations, and specifications are essential?
3. What series of steps do I have to follow to produce the output?
4. What am I going to make or produce?
5. Who am I going to serve, that is, who is going to get the output?

Glib, one-word answers aren't going to do the job here, of course. Even a small business needs to work hard to fully deal with the implications of *SIPOC*. The answer to Number 4, for instance, might not be just "pizza." What kinds of pizza? What sizes? Will you also make and sell sandwiches, other kinds of food, snacks, various kinds of drinks, and so on?

Now to our fourth excuse. What is being implied is that teachers will resist change and put up often insurmountable barriers to avoid facing it. Of course, if each and every teacher were doing an outstanding job, no one in his or her right mind would want them to change. The reality is, we know quite well, than it is change *for the better* that is being resisted, changes that will make teachers more effective educators.

The rationale for teacher evaluation, just like performance appraisal in a noneducational setting, is to get people to improve. Resistance, then, is clearly a way to stick to mediocrity and, maybe, to things even worse than that. So our question comes down to the evaluation process: How do we get teachers to see their value? And even more important, how do we make sure these evaluations actually *have* value? If we are going to use methods to evaluate teachers, how can we get them to really give us what we are after?

The first step is to identify all the groups or individuals that contribute to the process—our team (Suppliers). In order to address the claims of the tenure excuse there would certainly need to be representation from the school board, superintendent, principals, supervisors, and union leadership.

Next, these individuals would need to ensure that the evaluation processes being used to evaluate teacher performance comply at the very least with federal and state rules and regulations. More significantly, we have got to be sure that the critical features and standards of teaching excellence and ways of evaluating them are included in the process (Inputs).

Third is to make sure to identify all the key steps required in doing the evaluating from the preevaluation, the actual evaluation, and the postevaluation. Everyone has to know what, when, and how teacher evaluations will be conducted (Process). This is the heart of the matter, so to speak, since, although we are interested in getting individual teachers to do better, we are doing it in the name of standards that all teachers throughout the school and district have to meet. Standards are not individual, but *have to apply to all* in the system, while allowing, of course, for different ways to achieve them.

An art teacher will not have the same approaches that, say, a language or chemistry teacher has. Not only does fairness demand that evaluations be used consistently for everyone, but assurances that they are being so used will help to quell suspicions and other concerns. Illustrating the uniform process in a flow chart is one way to insure that this objective consistency is not someone's fantasy.

What are the outputs? Well, plainly, it's the aim of the whole process, and the team must specify in understandable language and with relevant measures what elements of teaching excellence will be evident and at work throughout the schools and district. The final step: the customers, clients, and all stakeholders (teachers, students, administrators, parents, guardians, community members) benefit from this highly effective evaluation process. This, when all is said and over, was the whole point of the project.

Notice how *SIPOC* forces one to consciously and deliberately think through *the what, why, and when of the steps in a project.* One can also see why some school districts[9] are wrapping the question about teacher classroom evaluation into the bigger picture of a *professional growth plan*. This methodological twist effectively puts the emphasis on professionalism, not on the potential for teachers seeing evaluations as another "Gotcha!" move to score points against them. It works on the premise that teachers not only want to do a good job, but want to get better and better at that job. Obviously, classroom success is critical to teaching value, but the broader development of educational professionals is also extremely important.

How does the *IDEAS* model fit in here, you might be thinking at this point. The key to the training for process identification and management is learning how to use the "A" in *IDEAS,* namely the tools we require to assess the results. And this necessitates that the process team and its educational leaders understand how to *identify and then track the measures and metrics that will confirm success or identify the areas for improvement.*

Charts and graphs are designed precisely for this purpose—at least when we use the right ones and use them correctly—and we mentioned earlier on how valuable they can be for communicating with all stakeholders in a school system. They tell us in a very effective, powerful, and unmistakable way how we are doing and what progress or lack of it is being made.

Some of the best schools and school districts we have worked with over the years make an extensive use of charts and graphs, in many cases publicly posting them throughout the buildings to show progress or the need to improve things like test scores, absenteeism, numbers of books read by students, and so on. Other charts, of course, especially those involving managerial and personnel matters, are reserved for those professionals and teams working with these issues. Whatever the area in

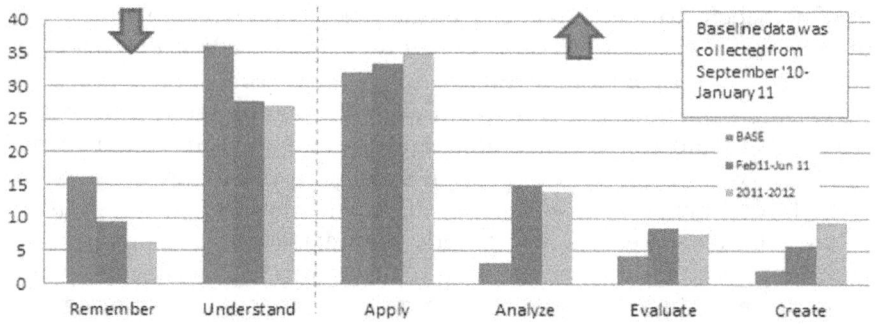

Figure 5.6.

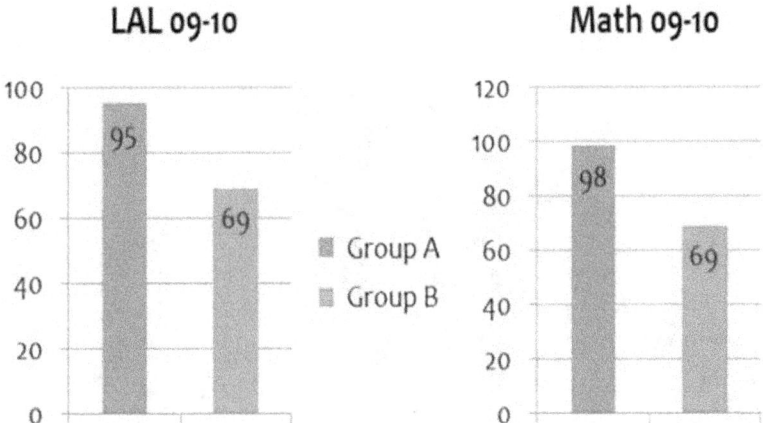

Figure 5.7.

which they are used, we stress the importance of understanding the roles and the uses of charts in our Academy sessions.

Here are just a few of the most frequently used charts and graphs that enable us to work more effectively with data-driven decision making. There is a lot to be said about them, and, although we do not have space to talk about them in great detail here, it can be valuable to have at least some familiarity with their broad outlines and uses.

Two different uses of the *Bar Chart* are shown in figure 5.6, and each quantifies the amount or frequency of occurrences in a given category by visually representing the relevant data using bars of different heights. These are very effective when comparing various data sets (figures 5.6 and 5.7).

When looking at only one set of data, the bars help us determine whether the data is normally distributed, that is, resembling the bell-shaped curve. We all remember that curve from our introductory courses in statistics, right? (If we were out of class that day, just understand that most of the incidents are in the "fat" upper part of the bell.) (See figure 5.8)

When we want to display this information in the order in which it occurred we use the *Control Chart*, which is more like a video than the bar chart, which is more of a snap shot. The control chart shown here is comprised of two parts: the lower chart tells us if we are measuring items that are alike, and the upper chart plots the individual measures over time. The dashed lines are referred to as control limits that reveal the degree to which our performance can very under normal conditions, but they need not concern us here. (See figure 5.9)

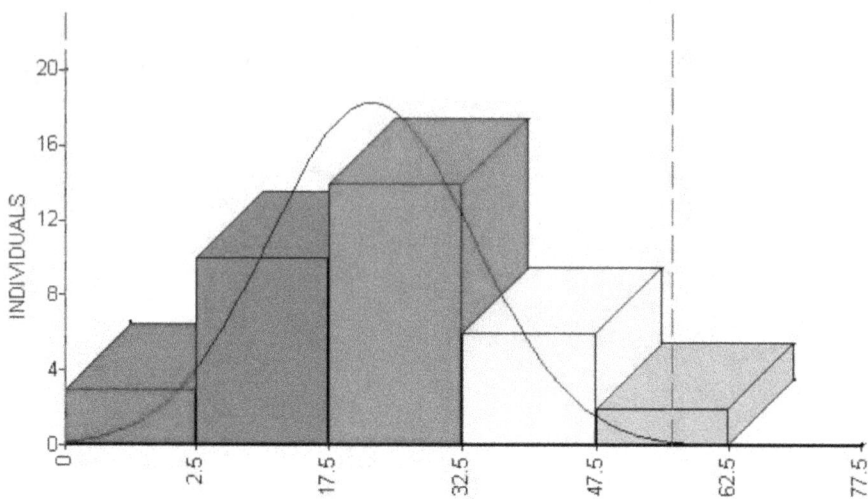

Figure 5.8. A Histogram with a Bell-shaped Curve

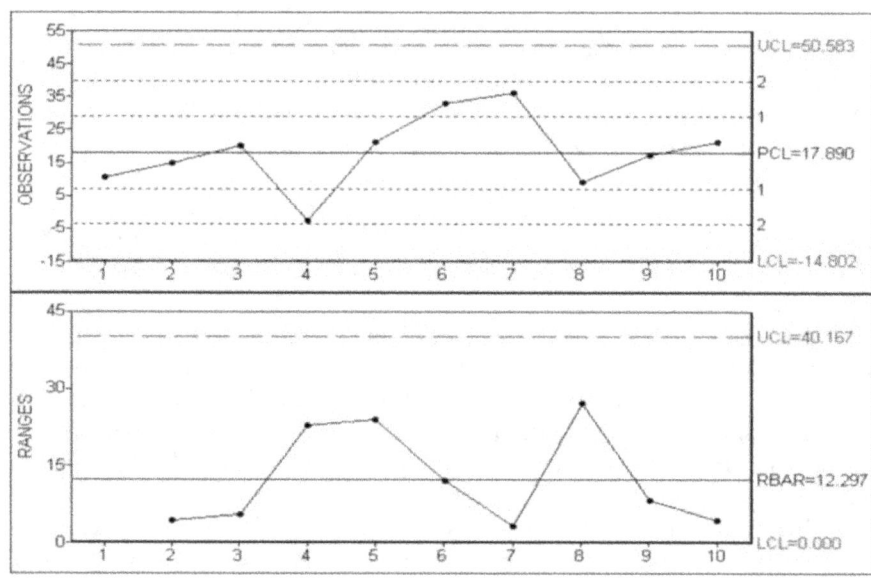

Figure 5.9. Typical Control Chart

When we find that the performance levels are unacceptable or that abnormal conditions exist, we look for the critical few variables that are causing the problems. This is our introduction to the *Pareto Diagram or Chart*. Many refer to it as the 70/30 or 80/20 Rule, but whatever you

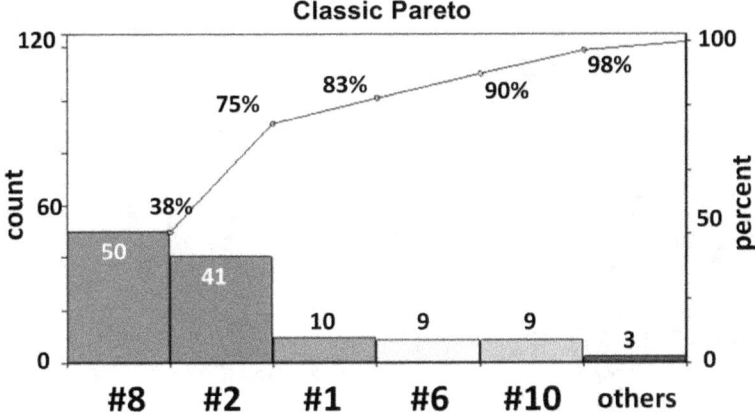

Figure 5.10.

choose to call it, the development of this chart is an integral part of the approach to using data to uncover root causes. (See figure 5.10)

Named for the great economist and engineer, Vilfredo Pareto, it uses both bars and line graphs and summarizes the relative importance of the differences between groups of data. The individual values are represented by the bars in descending order and the cumulative total is represented by the line.

The one chart shows that the Pareto principle reveals that most of the errors, or in this case the wrong answers, can be attributed to a critical few (20 or 30 percent) of all the possible sources. Focusing on the critical few will yield significant improvement.

The next chart demonstrates how one district's improvement team was able to identify that 80 percent of all office discipline referrals (ODRs) are the result of those individuals with four or more ODRs. Here again, if we address these critically few individuals, the majority of the overall problem will be resolved. (See figure 5.11)

Once the problems have been successfully addressed by attacking the root cause, the process must be monitored and or further evaluated to ensure a desired performance level is maintained or achieved. To that end a simple *Trend Chart*, such as the one shown below for tracking ODRs would help do the trick for us. (See figure 5.12)

When objective data is analyzed and charted it is very effective in pointing out the exact parts of the process that an individual excels in, as well as areas that may show an opportunity for some improvement. It is our very strong and verified belief that employees generally—whether teachers or those in any endeavor—want to excel. When presented with graphic data that is nonthreatening data, data is not merely a reflection of

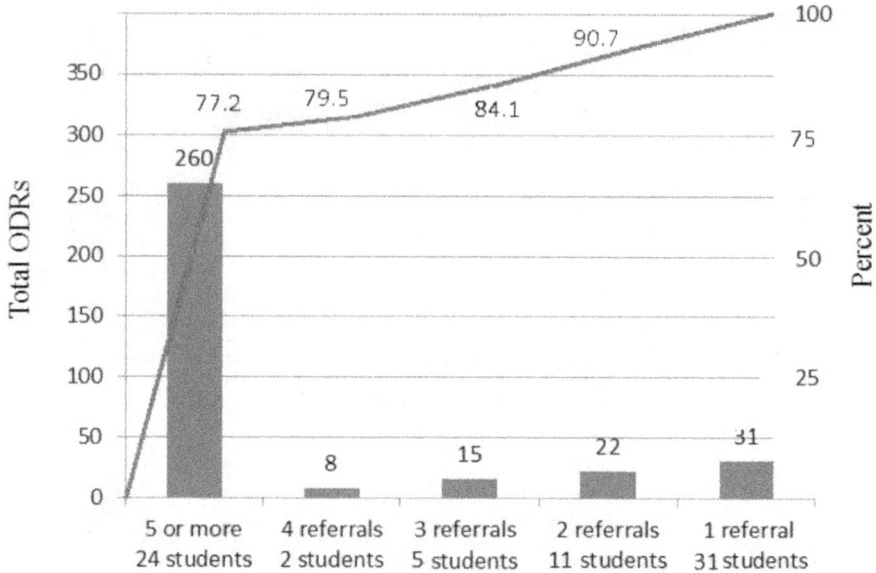

Figure 5.11.

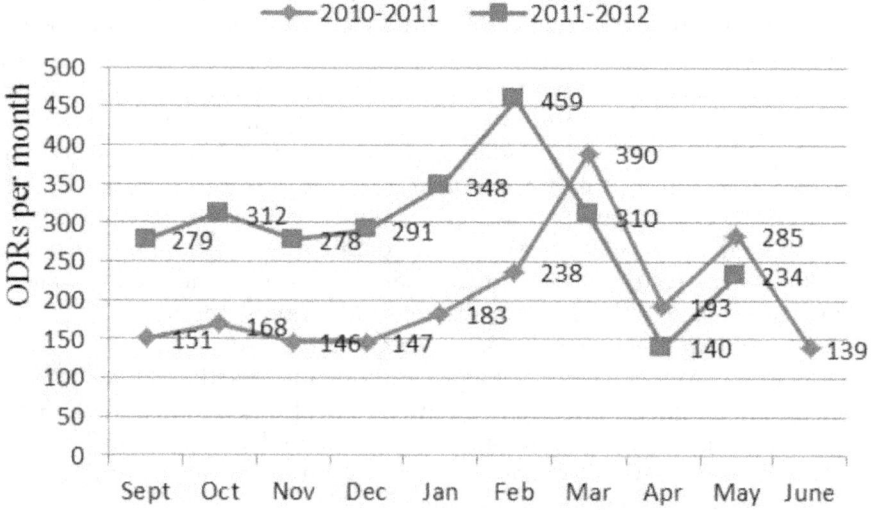

Figure 5.12.

the personal feelings or likes and dislikes of the evaluator, genuine impulses to improve and excel become ignited.

Let's remind ourselves about earlier points we made about change and the important way in which authentic leadership handles it. Most teachers are detailed learners who are comfortable with structure and consistency. They need to know that they will be successful in carrying out the traditionally tried-and-true teaching strategies. If an educational leader's goal is to have teachers significantly improve their approaches to instruction, then it is essential for them to understand that *teachers must be included in the analysis, evaluation, and deployment* of existing strategies.

This is where charting and other graphic means of illustrating a process have a major role to play, and educators should be trained in how to construct these and identify each of the critical steps in each process. The power of charts and graphs, among other things, is that it moves the discussion out of the private self and into the publicly accessible realm where all can look at it "out there."

We also know, of course, that teaching is an art as well as a science, and that great teachers can have very different individual styles. *SIPOC* and process thinking does not deny this. But if we are seeking to make sure that every child receives the same educational subject matter, receives it consistently and correctly, and that the teacher is using the most effective methods to insure student success, then concentration on the "science" side of teaching cannot be ignored. Vigorous and careful attention to the processes and substantive methods of good teaching with relevant measures and metrics leave plenty of room for personal style, just as scrupulous attention to good medical practice leaves lots of opportunity for doctors to develop individual ways to relate to patients.

Agreement on ways to improve based on good evaluations leads, quite naturally, to an *Action Plan* for making the improvement happen and helping assure that each teacher delivers the content using the same methodology and benchmarks. The Action Plan includes measures that track success throughout the school year as well as the end-of-the-year assessments. (See figure 5.13)

These in-process and outcome measures included in the Action Plan become the check points as well as the final proof of how much of the content the child has learned in the class. If the child is not meeting success at the determined check points then appropriate modifications are made well before the final assessments occur. Now the teachers know what data will be collected to determine success since they were involved in the development of the Action Plan. When teachers are treated like the professionals we want them to be and are involved in the things that matter to them most, namely effective teaching, which is their mission in life, they will generally *respond as professionals*. Anchoring this professional approach to *SIPOC* and Matrix Style Flow Charting can be the most powerful set of tools we have. (See figure 5.13)

One final word on charts and graphs. In addition to putting essential data into this form so it can be more easily made clear for evaluation and action, the very *visibility* of what is being charted or graphed takes it out of the realm of the personal and underscores its objectivity. It is there for

Problem Statement: *(a clear understanding of what needs to be solved)*
Goal Statement: *(the overall outcome this plan will make happen)*

OBJECTIVES	DUE DATE	ACTIONS	METRICS	RESPONSIBLE	REVIEW
Key steps towards achieving the goal	When it must be completed by	Specific or key strategies	How progress is measured	Who will lead & monitor progress	When progress will be reported

- Typically 3-5 [Objectives]
- Specific date(s) are best [Due Date]
- There are typically 1-3 for each Objective [Actions]
- Specific measures (#s/&s) or milestones [Metrics]
- Specific name(s) are best [Responsible]
- Specific date(s) prior to the due date [Review]

Figure 5.13. Typical Action Plan

all to see, to track, and to understand. It can no longer be considered the secret knowledge of a few special people, but public information to be worked on collaboratively. The charts and graphs, in essence, are another example of leadership credibility.

> EXCUSE NUMBER FIVE: Tenure makes good teaching about as valuable as acne.
>
> REPLY: The claim is not defensible.
>
> TOOL NEEDED: Communication and more effective professional assessment.

Tenure in and of itself is not the villain here, for if it were, as we noted previously, then there would be no good teachers who are tenured. Such a claim would be absolutely silly. Indeed, some school districts use as Master Teachers or Consulting Practitioners, precisely those with tenure who have proven how excellent they have been.

Nevertheless, revisions to tenure practices have been made in several states over the last few years, and more seem to be on the way. Rethinking any policy, whether educational or not, is generally a good thing, but much of this revision has been predicated on the belief that it is almost impossible to dismiss incompetent teachers who have tenure, coupled with the charge that strong teacher unions have handcuffed any administration that tries to change the status quo.

It turns out, however, that most of this is simply not true. In a study completed by Professor Perry Zirkel of Lehigh University's School of Education, school districts win cases against tenured teachers by a margin of three to one. In addition, the National Center for Education Statistics found that twice as many tenured teachers lost their jobs as nontenured teachers who were not renewed.[10]

Much of what we recommended in discussing the last excuse applies fairly directly to the tenure issue as well, and when administrators and supervisors blame tenure for poor teaching or other incompetence it is not unusual to find that there has been very little serious attention paid to treating teachers like professionals. The real issue generally comes down to ineffective evaluation techniques and tools, particularly in the probationary period during which teachers have not yet been given tenure.

If the aim of the process is to find fault, rather than work collaboratively to ensure a good outcome, it is hardly surprising that teachers themselves feel that their classroom observations are more akin to being a mongoose inspected by a cobra. The anxiety teachers have about evaluations, they often tell us, comes down to the inconsistent and ineffective evaluation process that exists in many schools today. The key to eliminating the excuse that tenure prevents good teaching is to be able to objectively use the "A" in *IDEAS*: Assess the Results produced by the evaluation process.

So we are back to *SIPOC* again, the process-centered, customer-driven approach that not only helps make sure we get a good outcome, but that we get it in the right way. We have stressed the importance of this above, particularly how it gets the discussion out of the murky woods of easily distorted feelings and individual sensitivities. In our reply to this excuse, however, we want to stress the critical importance of authentic leadership, especially the aspects connected with how leaders communicate.

The best leaders, we argued, develop a continuing questioning spirit and work to instill that spirit throughout the organization. If process thinking is at the source of meaningful teacher evaluations, then *what that process is, how it is intended to work, and how it can be challenged or improved* must be the primary goal of educational leadership. And that entails not that teachers are simply at the receiving end of the mandates for their evaluations, but are part of the team that puts the process together.

We have never understood, even after years of working with all types of schools and districts, why it seldom occurs to the leadership of a school or department to use the teachers as a major resource for building evaluation systems. And recent events in several states and cities in our country have shown that this critical point is still not being fully grasped in some quarters. Not only is doing this good policy from a collaborative point of view, but it allows you to get valuable ideas from the practitioners themselves. The rule here is about as absolute as anything ever gets in the universe of education: *in order to have an effective district evaluation process, the entire staff must be involved in its development and needs to be clear about how the process will be managed.* If the rule is followed, then at the conclusion of the process the right and relevant questions are encouraged by the leadership: Were the key requirements met? If so, to what degree? If not, why not and what can be done to get them met as soon as possible?

Notice how the issue of tenure becomes totally irrelevant now that we have focused on *process*. Just like our pizza shop example above where the aim is to make the best product, your customers will tell you soon enough if you've succeeded. If they aren't buying the pizza, you have to rethink what is wrong with the process, not what's wrong with them. We are all customers of many processes every single day, and on almost every one of those days we make judgments about how satisfied we are the quality of a product or service delivery.

We do this even in schools. No, we do it *especially* in school, since evaluative decision making is going on constantly. We pointed out earlier the central role that hiring and promotion practices play in a district's educational quality, whether these decisions are about teachers or administrators. The challenge to leadership is in structuring the reviews based on objective criteria that assess the levels of performance relative to a requirement(s). Failure to apply this fundamental principle can result in frustration, confusion, and a total breakdown of a leadership.

Again, a "real life" example:

A district superintendent that made the decision to hire a new principal over the strong objections of staff, some students, and interested community members, especially parents. Before long, despite the superintendent getting the go ahead from the school board, complaints began to pour in like a monsoon, causing several board members to put the hiring on hold pending a full review. The hurt feelings, injured egos, and resentments flew through the district like a wind storm, all based on the accusation that the superintendent had some personal agenda at work in the decision, not genuinely defensible reasons.

The superintendent, however, had actually used a process-oriented approach—a selection matrix through which he had evaluated all the applicants in terms of knowledge, skills, and abilities. He went before the board and tasked it to make its own selection using the same matrix, except with the names of the applicants removed. The board's results unanimously agreed with the superintendent's. One board member later apologized for appearing to undermine the process.

The lesson to be learned here? Yes, the superintendent is to be lauded for making an important decision using an objective and process-centered methodology. Yet he really needed a little work in the lessons of authentic leadership. For example, why did he not share the process he had used with the staff and other key stakeholders? In fact, why didn't he seek input from those stakeholders, especially the professional cadre, both in constructing the matrix and to get their take on how he ranked the applicants? Did he confuse his role as leader with the power trip good leaders must avoid? We have been repeating that the tools of systems thinking and process management are all—and essentially—*collaborative* tools. And authentic leadership is always about collaboration, because it is about making other leaders, not followers.

We are putting our soap box away . . . but just temporarily.

EXCUSE NUMBER SIX: School leaders are really terrible models of excellence.

REPLY: All right, let's discuss leadership again.

TOOLS NEEDED: More concentration on Authentic Leadership and its Vision.

Here is an interesting thought to grasp: educational leaders are really not that different from leaders in any industry or line of business. While those individuals who are fortunate enough to have work experience in the private sector prior to becoming an educator have little difficulty grasping this thought and its implications, those with only educational experience on their résumés might sometimes overstate this difference and, as we saw way back in Excuse Number One, conclude that the problems educational leaders face are very unlike those in other disciplines.

The difference between leadership in education and elsewhere comes down to this: *Absolutely Nothing*.[11] Leaders might sometimes be born, but that view is totally mythological and as a rule people need to learn and grow into the key elements of the practice of effective leading. That is why we prefer to present authentic leadership as a key series of *lessons*, not merely things to get up to doing without solid careful effort.

We know that there are many truly potentially good leaders, even great ones, who have not yet realized their opportunities. Ultimately, authentic leadership is, as we have been saying from our earliest pages in this volume, an essential element for a school or school district to attain high achievement for both students and staff. And the concentration on *IDEAS*, as we have also noted, is how authentic leaders work, since they live in the real world and manage by fact, not rumor or conjecture.

The "S" in *IDEAS* stands for, you will recall, standardizing the improvement. To standardize anything, of course, means to establish it in a way that makes it the rule, not a momentary fix that disappears and is quickly forgotten. Standardizing implies, then, that high performance is going to be a full-time resident at our place, not just an overnight visitor on its way somewhere else.

This last step in the process, however, clearly depends on the fact that everything that has gone before it has worked well. If the problem was misidentified or never clearly analyzed, if the root cause was misdiagnosed, the chances are that whatever solutions have been decided upon are not going to improve any performance, except, perhaps, by something akin to divine intervention. They are aimed at the wrong target, not the real cause of the problem that needs to be dealt with.

We have, unfortunately, witnessed more than one case of a school district truly and accurately pointing out to its public that it has instituted solutions x, y, and z only to find in the longer run that the problem still exists and might even be getting much more serious. The financial cost of these "solutions" can be considerable as well, and school boards and taxpayers quite naturally begin to demand some good answers.

Even in the odd case where an improvement did occur by some chance, few leaders of these districts can explain exactly what solution or strategy led to the improvement. Standardizing the improvement is not really possible, since no one is actually able to say what specifically brought it about. The principle at work here seems to be, "Shoot at everything that moves and take credit for everything that falls."

Authentic leaders, we know by now, constantly test assumptions by the logic of results, and the vision they communicate and inspire throughout the organization urges everyone to develop a serious questioning spirit to make sure that facts and analysis are the groundwork for any claims the organization has to rely on. They are constantly interested in making new leaders, not a group of disciples.

They show by actions that they understand that no one of us is smarter than all of us, provided all are thought of as key stakeholders in the successful life of the organization. Authentic leaders understand that the mission, vision, values, and goals of a school or other enterprise are not "top-down" monologues. They have to be shared and lived by everyone—teachers and other staff, school-board members, community leaders, and even students.

When authentic leaders standardize improvements they make doubly sure that everyone understands the demonstrable "why" of the new policy, procedure, or course of action, so that it is not viewed as a brainwave yanked out of thin air or the latest management theory craze. Nothing, in fact, gets implemented unless and until there is *clear established and demonstrable evidence* that the cause hindering the path to higher achievement is being addressed. Can it turn out to be wrong? Of course, but leaders respond to this situation not by looking for someone to blame or reaching into a bag of other excuses, but by focused and disciplined response.

A CASE IN POINT

A county technical school was experiencing an undeniably clear trend of declining enrollments, and as a result the school board gave the superintendent three district goals to be achieved in the coming school year: (a) increase enrollment and use of the school's facilities to the highest degree possible; (b) develop an adequate budget to make this happen; and (c) improve communication with the sending districts, including their communities, staff, and middle schools. The Performance Excellence Group was charged with training the school's leaders in how to systematically focus and streamline their efforts on these goals, including the identification and use of the key processes that would support getting these goals accomplished.

The superintendent, in collaboration with his cabinet set this vision: increase the school's enrollment by 5 percent, increase funding and the school's favorable status in the county. After analyzing relevant data carefully, they verified the trend in enrollment decline over the previous three years. Using several quality-improvement tools that included SIPOC and root-cause investigation, the team knew where to make changes that would have impact on the problem. Brainstorming to find the best potential solutions and strategies, the team settled on the following:

> *Key Strategy*: Create a district Steering Committee with several key professionals in the district.
>
> *Key Solution*: Charge the committee with developing and deploying a comprehensive marketing plan emphasizing recruiting students.

Perhaps this does not sound like a major development. Yet this was not the "death by committee" often mocked. The results were considerable and right on target for the goals. The Steering Committee established an atmosphere that fostered participation and creativity, helping school leaders at every level, including the classroom, to build consensus in planning for success and deploying strategies that ensured teamwork, accountability and a stakeholder-driven culture.

The tangible results? Enrollment grew by 6.5 percent, exceeding the target.

Other results? Significant savings in the cost of planning, a clear baseline data for establishing future trends, and an elevated reputation throughout the county.

Ineffective, nonauthentic leaders can show up in any business, any nonprofit . . . any human organization. When leaders speak their native language—the language of action—they not only get things done well but get them done with others in the organization. They become genuine models for others precisely because they do not confuse power with leadership. They focus on the job that has to be done, the problem that has to be solved, the improvement that has to be made and solidly implemented.

Schools and districts have to insist on and invest in leadership development at every level. We are not speaking of the kind of "leadership" courses that are really programs teaching administrators how to survive in tough times. Survival is not the aim of good leaders. And the investment in authentic leadership is money and time very well spent because it has a multiplying effect throughout the enterprise.

EXCUSE NUMBER SEVEN: School Board Policy Will Destroy Every One of us Anyway.

REPLY: If you really believe this, it's probably time to shop for another career.

TOOLS NEEDED: The road map for the Journey to high-achieving schools.

We'll start this discussion by painting a picture of what some of you might think is so idyllic that we could be telling a story about events in the Enchanted Forest. We can assure you, however, that we have seen the ideal approached more than once, if not perfectly, than at least with serious and measurable progress.

The school board is responsible to assure that the school district fulfills its mission, a purpose mandated by federal and state rules and regulations as well as by the needs of its community. Boards function at the highest level of the district, monitoring the strategic plan of the district as well as fulfilling the fiduciary role for the community. They are required to make sure all policies are current and meet or exceed state and federal regulations as well as the requirements of all its stakeholders.

Some school boards believe that the community selects or elects them to actually run the district. That is not only incorrect, but can lead to disaster on many fronts. The most effective boards understand that they serve as the governing body whose principal job is to understand and honestly represent the needs of the community and oversee the current condition of the school district. Schools boards are the monitors of all the policies, finances, and the strategic plan of the school district, and among their chief responsibilities is the search for and selection of a Chief Education Officer to implement the district's strategic and operational plans that cohere with the values of the community.

The relationship between a well-run school board and the district superintendent is that between a corporate or nonprofit board and its CEO. In the ideal situation the board works with the CEO to develop a "dash board" of indicators that reflect the key goals and objectives of the district's strategic plan, which can be tracked and reported to the board on a regular schedule. In the best cases the "dash board" is not kept as a private piece of "classified" information, but is regularly communicated to the professional staff and the community at large on websites and in other ways as it should be.

It follows, therefore, that in the best school boards, members are very skillful in asking the right kinds of questions, inquiries that elicit factual information and data showing both that the district is making the relevant kind of progress, and is also in compliance with the regulatory and financial requirements. Serving on a school board is among the most challenging public-service jobs one can have, since it involves not only opening a meaningful future of the children in the district's charge, but responding to the needs of citizens, administrators, teachers, and state and regional regulators.[12] In an ideal situation, and despite the fact that members come from all walks of life and bring with them different values and personalities, they are nevertheless able to reach consensus and work with the CEO in order to achieve the mission, vision, values, and goals of the district. The superintendent, as an authentic leader, encourages board questioning, just as he or she promotes and, if fact, demands it throughout her or his entire staff.

The key process that is essential to get this kind of relationship between the school board and CEO is a model that illustrates the big picture of how the district will implement its strategic, operational, and other major plans, and how it will maintain the already established successes as well as pursue new opportunities for improvement. What is needed is something that can focus and direct everyone in the school district to the same essential end, something that clears out the politics and short-sighted attitudes that result in actual harm to students in the long (and not so long) run.

THE JOURNEY TO HIGH-ACHIEVING SCHOOLS

In our discussion of the excuses we tried to show some specific quality tools, lessons, and lines of attack to help eliminate the presumed basis for the excuse. These approaches were not random actions picked out of the air, but are actually elements of a comprehensive model that we have developed over a ten-year period working with numerous school districts of several different kinds.

This model is called *The Journey to High-Achieving Schools* (JTHAS™). When this model is shown, explained, and discussed with school boards, staff, and members of the community, it forms the nucleus of an opportunity to reach consensus on how the entire school community can work together to accomplish the highest student achievement possible. This model creates reasonable and fair checks and balances for each segment

88   Chapter 5

of the school district and key stakeholders in the community, fostering an environment where integrity and credibility can replace mistrust, blame, and the resort to excuses. If the model is used as it should be used, and given some dynamic leadership at several levels in the district, especially in the CEO's office, the potential for the district becoming world class is not a fantasy.

JTHAS™ is not only a roadmap by which leaders can address countless challenges, but it can it facilitate the embracing of a philosophy and actual standardized practices of continuous improvement, including the solving of crucial problems, building consensus and developing creative and productive teams. Leaders systematically learn how to focus and streamline their efforts, identify key processes in need of improvement, and deploy project teams whose players focus on delivering significant and measurable process improvements.

Following the model also teaches leaders and others how to challenge the status quo in a disciplined and useful way, and to seek out the best practices that increase stakeholder and staff satisfaction. More than increasing capacity, these skills can truly be life-altering.

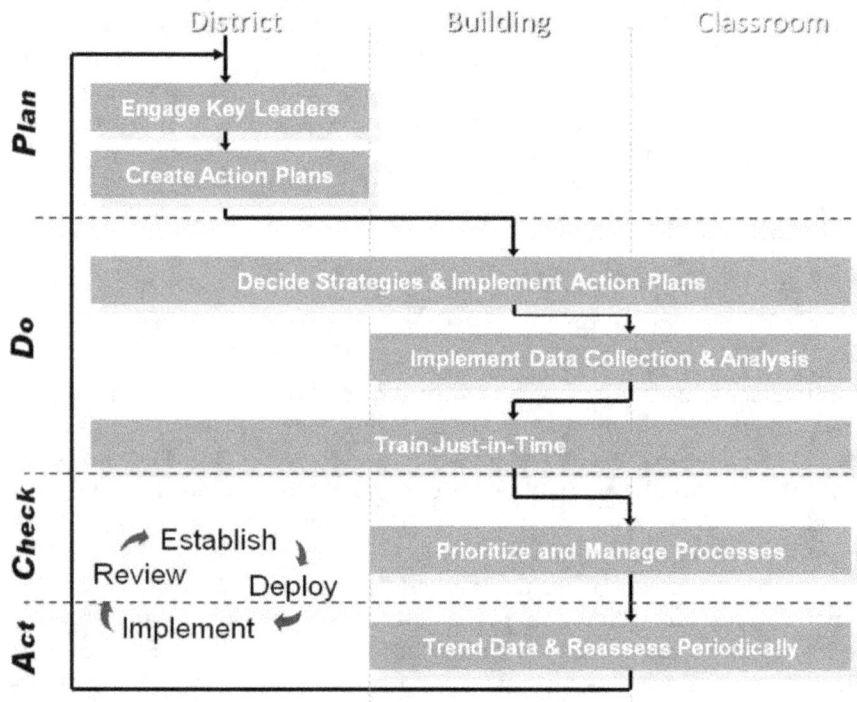

Figure 5.14.   The Journey to High-Achieving Schools

The model, however, is not a one-size-fits-all affair, since every leader is not identical to every other and school districts do not come out of a cookie cutter. For JTHAS™ to perform in ways that make significant progress, interventions on a leader-by-leader basis are always required, not just for the CEO but for the entire leadership of the district. By customizing the implementation of the model, leadership can be more secure in knowing that the new skills and capabilities are solidly maintained. JTHAS™ is not a panacea, but a tested road map. Some roads, of course, are rockier and trickier than others.

IDEAS AT WORK: ONE DISTRICT'S EXPERIENCE

We'll conclude our examination of excuses by showing an application of the *IDEAS* process in a district we have been working with. The district's experience might help illustrate several things. First, how a systems approach can not only address a specific set of issues, but can work to make a difference in the outlook of the professional staff. It also shows how the process can work with other strong educational tools to make their use even more effective. Along the way we will also see how the temptation to fall back on some of the excuses we have been considering can be addressed as well.

The general problem—actually a set of problems—involved the question of why students weren't learning, as evidence on several relevant measures, including test scores, was plainly revealing. The district is a challenging one to manage. The town's median household income is well below the state average, for example, has a significant number of home mortgages in trouble, and is in a county where the homeless have become a major policy issue.

The district began its journey by piloting an approach using quality improvement concepts at both the elementary- and high-school levels. They learned and worked through the *IDEAS* process identifying a problem, looking for root causes, exploring possible solutions, and implementing those solutions in a structured and focused way. Finding that there was clear merit to the process they had begun there, the district expanded its efforts to another elementary and high school.

It yielded some results, but they were still disappointingly limited, since not everyone within a building was seeing the same level of improvement. It started to become clear that the processes were not being communicated or implemented in a uniform way.

The superintendent, after intensive meetings with her cabinet and with help from the Performance Excellence Group, concluded that what was lacking, not just in those schools not using the improvement strategies but also in those that already were, was a demonstrable *commitment* to *academic rigor* in the classroom. This conclusion was not a matter of "gut feel" but was based on the data from classroom observations.

Academic rigor—understood to be strong inquiry-based learning, with more emphasis on problem solving, development of analytical thinking skills, greater stress on writing that cuts across all disciples, and in general more in-depth content on all subject matter—was simply not being seen uniformly and systemically in the educational process.

The district set out on a course to ensure that *Classroom Instruction That Works* (CITW, one of the most widely used research-based professional-development manuals) became the lynchpin in the objective to markedly increase academic rigor. *Plan-Do-Check-Act* obviously needed to be at the center of the thinking here, since a strategic action plan had to be in place. It had to be one that clearly defined who was going to do what, by when, what indicators of progress were going to used, and how the plan was going to be monitored to make sure things were on course and being implemented.

The plan was ambitious and district-wide, aimed at being implemented in every building, at every grade in every classroom. The deployment process also required each building administrator to be held accountable for implementing his or her own action plans showing how the plan would be installed. The school superintendent and each building administrator would also be responsible for adopting the means by which data could be systematically collected, analyzed, and reviewed on a periodic basis.

No quick fix was anticipated, since it was clear that that evidence of progress on improved learning and outcomes from the CITW strategies in every classroom and in every building would surely take time and not magically happen overnight. Providing training was the first step. This was done in accordance with a carefully developed decision procedure to select the best training product (also from the developer of the CITW) followed by and an action plan to implement it. Although there was a change in superintendent leadership as the training progressed, the new superintendent chosen had already worked with the Performance Excellence Group's *Journey to High-Achieving Schools* model and fully understood the systems-thinking approach to educational improvement. One of his first priorities was to track the academic rigor effort to see if it made a difference in classroom learning.

A key thing to underscore is that the new CEO appreciated the critical importance of having the support of the community and the leadership at the highest levels of the district, especially the board of education. So he worked with the board to explain the process, why it was important, and the specific strategies that would be used to get the district moving in the right direction.

The board enthusiastically agreed with the initiative and, quite logically, agreed to use the results as one of the evaluative measures of both the district's progress and the superintendent's performance. The presentation to the board, by the way, was just the first of several throughout the year to report on the progress of the academic-rigor initiative throughout the district. The meetings were supported by relevant data, which was illustrated by charts and graphs that represented progress on the initiative. It became even more clear as this data was analyzed that students' higher-order thinking skills were an area that still remained in need of more effective attention.

This district consciously made regular and effective communication one of its main priorities, especially communication with its teachers. The leadership understood that since regular walkthroughs by supervision were now going to be an essential part of the normal landscape, many teachers would be understandably concerned with what kinds of data in the classroom observations were going to be considered relevant, how the data would be used, and what safeguards were in place to make sure that the entire program was professionally driven.

At the monthly leader meetings, therefore, there was constant attention paid to these issues to allay as many of these fears as possible, especially to explain that all data would be reviewed and carefully analyzed. Eventually, many teachers related that they looked forward to being observed, but the credibility and trust in the fairness of the process had to be earned over time. Underscoring it as crucially connected with the professional development of teachers began to make a difference.

It became more and more understandable that the system in place was geared to *objective, measurable data*, not to personalities, and that the classroom observations were an essential part of professional responsibility for making educational progress.[13] The central message was that the responsibility was being taken seriously and was absolutely incompatible with shortcuts or slapdash reports. Things began to change for the better, gradually but significantly.

Administrators did not welcome the change enthusiastically at first either. The initial primary indicator used to track the progress of the initiative was the number of walkthroughs conducted. While many administrators openly commented early on that conducting ten of these a week would be quite challenging, they soon concluded that they were easily meeting this target. Although it took some time to make sure that the data being reported in the observations was giving a fair picture of the classroom instruction, the walkthroughs were revised upward to twenty-five per week when it became clear that each teacher needed the additional observations so the collected data could be more accurately validated.

Of course, the bottom line for all of this was about improving student achievement. While there is still much to be done, gains definitely have been made, and information that teachers and administrators have about the measurement of those gains is consistently shared with the school board. Good systems thinking requires constant scrutiny of the processes we use, so questions still need to be addressed. What level should student performance actually achieve to count as genuine improvement? How do we connect student achievement with specific kinds of instructional techniques? What variables need to be included or excluded and on what rational basis?

WHAT THE CASE SHOWS

There is, we believe, a great deal that many of us can learn from this district's experience as it worked and continues to put its challenging plans into place. Think, for example, about how it *met and overcame many of the destructive excuses* we have been addressing, reasons some districts have used for giving up the quest for higher achievement. Among some key points to take note of:

- Instead of concluding that the kind of process thinking that can make a real difference in other disciplines had no role to play in education, this district embraced the idea totally and seriously.
- It did not blame students for lack of educational progress, but looked to its own policies and practices and how they could be improved.
- The introduction of change was not viewed as a reason to give up the pursuit of improvement, but a challenge to be met carefully by first-rate and constant communication.
- The board and community were not painted as obstacles to progress, but partners in the endeavor to make the schools better.
- Both tenured and nontenured teachers and administrators developed action plans, identified and aligned specific action measures, and reviewed charts and graphs in support of the observations of classroom instruction.
- The superintendent and supervision consistently showed authentic leadership by building credibility and trust throughout the district, especially in the professional ways in which the staff was treated.
- It has connected its mission, vision, values, and goals into a mindset where systems thinking and authentic leadership are giving everyone more focus and discipline, where surface and substance are not confused, and where the true arbiter of progress has become objective fact, not shadowy feeling.

There is no doubt that the district is seeing improvement where it matters, but is also in a much better position to make further progress than it has ever been in its past. Nor should it be surprising that the more information that was shared with the teachers and administrators in this process, the better deployed and more effective the strategies became.

The leaders in this initiative demonstrated by their actions that it is not only possible to develop and set out a workable plan of measurable improvement for every classroom throughout the district, but it also showed that there was great value in so doing. The central office kept setting a solid example throughout the district, getting supervisors and department heads to see the strategy as their own, not imposed from on high. As a result, when issues arose connected with not meeting targets, the atmosphere was generally the collegial one of how to overcome obstacles, not about finding ways to assign blame to other individuals.

This is a very good position to be in.

IDEAS FOR FURTHER CONSIDERATION

Here are some points that might be helpful in using the *IDEAS* process:

Key Things to Remember for the "I" In IDEAS

- You must begin by making your problem visible in an actionable statement.
- If you already know the cause of the problem, ask, "Is this worth pursuing?"
- If the problem is not one that has significant impact on your mission, vision, values, or goals, ask, "Is this worth pursuing?"
- The Problem Statement has to be specific, measurable, objectively stated, show the gap between where things actually are and where they should be, and point to the pain or negative impact if the problem is not addressed.
- Do not settle for your first or even second version of the Problem Statement, but distribute it for review and full discussion, so that good questions about it can be asked and so it can be made more useful for the rest of the *IDEAS* process.

Key Things to Remember for the "D" In IDEAS

- When beginning the process to determine the root cause, understand that your objective is *not* to find a solution to the problem, but rather to seek out the cause that needs to be addressed with a solution to be determined later.
- You are after the root cause, not just anything that might affect the problem or make it worse, so keep asking "Why?" as many times as needed to get to the bottom of the suggested candidate.

In suggesting possible causes for the problem, ask yourself if you have a data-based reason for the suggestion or if you are merely relying on earlier assumptions.

Brainstorm as many possible causes as you can, arrange them in categories and eliminate duplicates; do not at this stage (generating ideas) argue, analyze, or defend ideas.

Use a structured process to rate your top possible causes so you can arrive at the most likely candidate.

If you still need additional data to substantiate that your most likely root cause is at work, plan a process for getting it.

Key Things to Remember for the "E" in IDEAS:

Brainstorming and full discussion are the best ways to get a range of ideas about what solution or solutions might best address the cause of the problem.

Narrow the solutions to a controllable number by using the Nominal Group Technique or some other structured process for rating the possibilities.

Have clear and visible criteria against which to evaluate the possible solutions, such as cost-to-benefit ratio, feasibility, compatibility with other processes already at work in the organization, and so on.

For higher cost solutions, consider a pilot or test version of the solution to reduce the risk of financial exposure.

Avoid multiple solutions being tried concurrently since there will be no clear way to establish which of the solutions actually addressed the cause.

Key Things to Remember for the "A" in IDEAS

The "A" is for "action" as well as "assessment"; therefore you must work to put an Action Plan in place to get the solutions implemented.

Action planning, like all the *IDEAS* processes, absolutely requires collaboration and full discussion. It must not be done in isolation or in a top-down way.

The goals and objectives in the plan must be clear and be specific, measurable, achievable, relevant, and time-bounded.

Good Action Plans clearly and unambiguously specify who is going to do what, by when, with whom, and how and when the progress on the plan will be reviewed.

As the Plan is deployed, objective monitoring of how well the application of the solutions have been working is required. *Plan-Do-Check-Act* should be the rule.

Can These Things Work in Any School? Even Mine? You're Kidding!   95

As much as possible, illustrate the processes at work in the Action Plan with charts and graphs to make the processes involved easier to keep track of and show where any difficulties might arise as things progress.

A productive if not very comforting thought to keep handy is that there could be other causes of the problem than the one or ones you have decided upon.

Key Things to Remember for the "S" in IDEAS

If the results shown in deploying the Action Plan seem positive, you must find a way of showing how they have begun to close the gap in the Problem Statement.

You will need (both for yourself and others) data to show that the gap is being addressed; without such data, your claim of progress will be seen as mere conjecture.

To be sure that the gap closer is not illusory or a one-shot deal, make sure there is enough time to get changes accomplished and/or that other variables have not been introduced in the process unknowingly.

Give a good deal of consideration to making sure—through good communication and support—that the effective solution(s) to the problem are truly standardized by making them into normal operating procedure.

Celebrate the efforts and success of everyone involved in the initiative.

Now, How about Giving It a Try?

We think it is important that the educational leaders who have been working through the issues discussed in the previous pages begin to try their hand at the *IDEAS* model as soon as they can and put together teams to address the following questions.

1. What is a major problem that your school or school district is facing, a problem for which the cause is not known (even if suspected) and which is having a serious impact on the quality of education? Put this problem into an actionable statement using the *SMOG*(p) technique. Discuss each element of the technique, asking questions regarding the statement's specificity, the possibility of smuggling in a solution, how the gap in the present and future should be described or measured, and so on. Do not settle for the first written version of the problem statement, but review it again during at least one additional meeting. Remember: if the problem statement is not clear, nothing else in the process will be clear.

2. Use the brainstorming methods and guidelines described in the last chapter to discuss the potential root causes of the problem. Again, ask questions about the clarity and the specificity of the suggested candidate causes. Are they really possible causes or merely areas of further concern about the problem? Keep asking "Why?" to make sure.
3. What are some ideas your team can advance to address the causes that have been suggested to be at the root of the problem? How would you rate them in terms of cost, feasibility, effectiveness, and your team's capability to address them effectively? Discuss why you believe any of them could eliminate or reduce the effect the causes are having. How would you arrange to test any of them without committing too many vital resources in case you are wrong?
4. Without developing a full-scale Action Plan—at least not yet—begin by listing three to five things that have to get done to get the solutions up and running. Who is responsible for getting them started? Who else might help with the effort? How will you know that progress on the action is actually going to be made?

NOTES

1. The model in the educational case tends to be described as *Plan-Do-Study-Act* to put more emphasis on the need for beginning with and coherently addressing the data that revealed the problem.

2. One of the key resources we use and stress in our *Academy for Education Leaders* is one of the best models of systems thinking, namely, *Educational Criteria for Performance Excellence (2011–2012)* published by the Baldrige Performance Excellence Program. The program is managed by the US Department of Commerce National Institute of Standards and Technology. Information about the book and more about the Baldrige Program can be found at www.nist.gov/baldrige.

3. The great Greek philosopher named Aristotle also once noted that a little mistake in the beginning of a process can become a major disaster by the time you get to the end.

4. A very useful analysis of the concepts at the heart of this claim and related ones can be found in an article by M. Donald Thomas and William L. Bainbridge, "All Children Can Learn: Facts and Fallacies." The full text can be found at schoolmatch.com/articles/PDKMay01.htm.

5. Dr. Brian Daly, a psychologist at Drexel University in Philadelphia, recently pointed out to us that just as this conflict of temperaments can lie at the root of parent–child clashes, so it often forms the basis for teacher–student difficulties. The more aware we are of the personality traits of both parties, the more likely is the possibility that mismatches can be more effectively handled for better outcomes.

6. These techniques and the other methods we will be discussing in the next pages work very effectively with students, not just those seeking to determine why they do not seem to respond or be motivated. A study reported by The Center for Public Education—*Defining a 21st Century Education* (Craig D. Jerald, July 2009)—notes that among the kinds of knowledge and skills that most benefit students for the future are the ability to think critically about information, solve novel problems, communicate and collaborate, create new products and processes, and adapt to change. Perhaps

great educational leaders and great teachers already know this. The key question—in large part the mission of this book—is why are we so seldom doing all we can to make sure it is happening? Cf. centerforpubliceducation.org/Learn-About/21st-Century.

7. A valuable source on multivoting and other consensus techniques is the website of the American Society for Quality at asq.org/learn-about-quality.

8. We will say more about this process when we discuss Excuse Number Four below.

9. For example, Montgomery County in Maryland. Both general and more specific information is available at montgomeryschoolmd.org/info/baldrige/leadership/improvements/htm.

10. Valerie Strauss, "The Myth of Teacher Tenure," *Washington Post*, July 13, 2010. voices.washingtonpost.com/answer-sheet/teachers/the-myth-of-teacher-tenure.html.

11. See, for example, F. J. Abbate, "Education Leadership in a Culture of Compliance," *Phi Delta Kappan* 91, no. 6 (March 2010): 35–37.

12. Two of the authors of this volume have served on school boards, so this statement is not a platitude for us.

13. What gets measured, we know, gets done. And what gets measured well gets done well.

SIX

Every Journey Has a Few Potholes: Here's Some Help in How to Handle Them

We have forty million reasons for failure but not a single excuse. —Kipling

The mayor in a small town in New Jersey some years ago realized that his budget had pretty much run its course and the coffers for public works projects were just about empty. In particular there was absolutely no money left to repave a major township road that was in especially appalling shape. It was covered from end to end with potholes, ruts, and serious skull-numbing fissures.

His solution was quite simple. One morning signs appeared at either end of the road with the message: "Drive Slowly—Rough Road Ahead." When asked about his decision, he claimed that it was a model of public policy for which he should be lauded. After all, he had not only saved the taxpayers money on the resurfacing costs, but had also made great progress on public safety by helping reduce speeding in the town.

Creative politics aside, the idea of such a sign is not a bad idea for those who start the difficult journey to becoming a high-achieving school. We know that the highway has got to be taken if we are going to get to our destination, and we might even be able to glimpse hazily what is at the end of it. Yet we also have to be aware that it is not going to be a smooth ride for much of the way. Understanding this clearly won't save your tax dollars like the mayor, of course, but expecting to meet some resistance can prepare you for a safer, if somewhat slower drive.

What are some of these "potholes" or obstacles that have to be addressed to which we refer? Here are some of the most significant ones that have appeared over the years in our experience with school leaders:

a. Frustration, since the new processes initially seem awkward and complicated;
b. Expecting quick fixes and magic bullets;
c. Believing that good is . . . well, really just good enough;
d. Being "finish-driven" rather than "data-driven";
e. Playing the Blame Game to justify the lack of progress;
f. Forgetting that any organization is not one thing, but many things;
g. Looking for conspiracies at work that are sabotaging the effort;
h. Valuing fire fighting over fire prevention; and
i. Blurred vision.

Before we start taking a closer look at these culprits, let's again repeat a point that has probably hit a new monotony record for some of the educators who have been working their way through this book:

Leadership that is strong, effective, credible—in a word, authentic—is the necessary ingredient for addressing these impediments on the journey to high achievement. The tools we have been talking about in all the earlier pages are collaborative tools, not methods to be used in isolation from the school's or district's on-the-ground reality. Authentic leaders, we have said, foster a questioning spirit throughout the organization, emphasize and illustrate strong values, and aim constantly to promote genuine freedom and innovation.

To announce, for example, that the administration is developing an action plan for a particular program, and that the results will be communicated to the faculty and staff at some future date is a *modus operandi* that has "Guaranteed Failure" written all over it in large neon lettering. When the schools or other organizations we have worked with fall short in making real progress toward a culture of excellence, it is not that they lack the ability to use the tools. Generally the reason for the letdown is that they needed to pay much more attention to the leadership environment and the value culture in which those tools are to be used. We will, of course, be saying more about this as we move our "pothole" brigade along.

THE FRUSTRATION FACTOR

Anyone who has ever begun to learn a new language, a musical instrument, or a sport requiring physical movements new to the learner clearly understands that there is a kind of "abnormality" to the learning enterprise. It is not simply that things are *different* as you keep checking your moves against the recommended methodology; things actually seem *unnatural*, and even at times downright annoying.

The temptation, therefore, to fall back into our comfort zone of earlier habits gets stronger, especially since many educational leaders have long experience with their traditional approaches and have not made a bad job of using those customary tactics to address issues.

Some things to keep in mind:

First, *believe* that using these tools and the leadership skills required to make them part of your culture have been used successfully by others and that genuine, measurable progress has been made in hundreds of cases. The trick is to begin by using the methods on a problem or for problems that are not global or strategic, not what Jim Collins in *Good to Great* calls BHAGs, "Big Hairy Audacious Goals." Start with manageable issues where you and your team can gain some familiarity with the processes and see some measurable outcomes.

Second, the use of the process tools we have been recommending does not—repeat—*does not negate your existing expertise* and experience. On the contrary, it would be impossible to cancel it out, since the tools absolutely require your existing solid knowledge so they can be used effectively. Your familiarity and understanding of educational practice as an experienced professional is vital and cannot be ignored.

For example, you will need to determine with your colleagues things such as what major problems need to be acted on, what are the relevant gaps that need to be looked into, where the root causes might lie, and what solutions are truly practical for making real progress on dealing with those causes. Systems thinking does not replace your hard-won learning and experience. It helps to powerfully *focus* that learning so that meaningful and measurable steps toward improvement can be made. Total amnesia is not only not required, but will almost certainly result in disaster.

Third, remember our earlier discussion of change and how it is received and reacted to by most people in most organizations. Major new ways of thinking and the standards by which they will be evaluated have to be *introduced gradually*, have to be fully and meaningfully explained, and absolutely necessitate patience and understanding. Everyone who is involved with the change process needs time and support before matters start running smoothly. Leaders, recall, need to bring out the right stuff in their teams; they must not try to stuff them full of right.

MAGIC BULLET MYTHS

This pothole is related to the frustration issue, but deserves some separate comment since it can lead in some very odd directions. Many of us, we would guess, have heard the humorous maxim, "When everything else fails, read the instructions." Reading the instructions seems to take time that we don't have much of any more as life is becoming increasingly filled with expectations for very quick answers to just about any question. Waiting even two or three seconds for a website to come up on our computer screens is considered by some—include your authors at times—to be absolutely unacceptable.

Often some participants in our Academy sessions seek immediate results from using the process tools, once they appreciate how truly powerful they can be. The temptation, therefore, is to start using them without making sure that all the important bases have been covered. These imperative bases include being clear about the problem statement, especially guarding against building in (sometimes in very subtle ways) assumptions about the root cause or dismissing some practical solutions without careful discussion.

In addition, these tools, we keep stressing, work most powerfully when they are used in a collaborative way, and teamwork and a cooperative approach take patience and time. Rushing the process will generally lead to mistakes—usually mistakes that are seldom insignificant ones.

We also know that there can be something a bit exhilarating about the intellectual appeal of the process, and this, too, can be at root of the pothole here. It is certainly important for administrators and other leaders to share what has been learned about systems thinking and how it can effectively address critical educational issues. The process is not, however, merely an abstract and intellectual exercise, but one that has to be internalized and applied.

No magical things can happen by merely talking with others in the school or district about what one has learned. The process has to be experienced in *concrete application*. We always advise the participants in our Academy, for example, to work an actual problem confronting their school or district and to apply the leadership and key elements of *IDEAS* to it so that real results can be demonstrated. The results are the best teaching tools for others in the district, not the mere parroting of theoretical concepts.

The connection with our earlier difficulty should also be clear. When the quick fix or magic bullet fails to do the job, frustration is bound to set in. And, of course, the temptation to fall back into our earlier comfort zone becomes very hard to resist. Like wildfire, the judgment that the process "really can't work here" spreads throughout the entire district, and whatever gains made will be lost. Fight this temptation as strongly as you can by realizing that you are actually making progress by using the tools deliberately and carefully. Excellence does not happen in one full sweep or one fell swoop.

THE "GOOD ENOUGH" SYNDROME

One of our major aims in the previous pages is to show how excuses destroy the very foundations of a culture of excellence in education, as they do in almost any organization. We have sometimes seen educators use the skills of authentic leadership and the powerful tools of systems thinking to achieve some small improvements, but then come to believe that those improvements are the best levels that can be attained. In short, this is simply another way of falling into the trap of the excuse-riddled mindset. The original meaningful vision erodes into a hallucination, not because it is an overly ambitious and grandiose delusion, but, on the contrary, because it has subtly mutated into a narrow and small-minded goal easily achieved by almost anyone.

Successful leadership does not find reasons to deflate the vision, for the vision is the critical framework against which we must judge all of our major decisions. Authentic leaders, we know, have a questioning spirit, and one of the most important questions they ask—and keep asking—is:

"How does what we are proposing to do by this significant decision, policy or practice get us closer to our vision as an organization, closer to what we all aspire to become?"

If the answers approximate responses such as: (1) "We don't know," or (2) "We're not sure," or (3) "It doesn't actually get us any closer but doing so will require a great expenditure of time, energy, and other resources, and we're not sure we want to go that route," the conclusion should be as clear as the most transparent crystal: "Then why in the name of all that is Excellence are we even thinking about it?"

Not every decision, of course, will be evaluated in terms of the vision. The dozens of judgments made every day in a school district are often fairly routine, although they all should be made in accordance with the lessons of good leadership. It is crucial, however, not to lose sight of the vision-framework, even in decisions that seem of little moment, for they might show a pattern taking the district down the wrong path if we do not review them periodically. The more solid gains should be thought of as important mileposts on the journey to higher achievement, not as excuses to stop progress. We celebrate them, learn from them, and use them as stepping stones to move to even higher achievement.

To avoid the temptation to settle for less than excellence in our practices, it might be a good thing to imagine this scenario: how comfortable you would be with a physician who tells you that she hasn't got the time or energy to completely rid you of your curable health problem. What she will do, however, is just enough to make you feel a lot better. Of course, you will still be very, very sick, but at least some good has come out of the encounter, hasn't it? Any questions?

DAMN THE FACTS—FULL SPEED AHEAD!

We encounter this pothole when we push to get to a resolution of a problem or the deployment of a plan no matter what the facts, figures, or other data actually show. Unlike the temptation of settling for "good enough," this syndrome seems to understand that small victories are not sufficient, so let us, we guess, give it credit for at least that much. Yet, in the well-intentioned pursuit of pushing the school or district to a level of higher achievement, this approach will not take any prisoners, nor allow prickly facts to get in the way of progress.

It is certainly understandable to want to resolve a problem that appears to be keeping the organization back from excellence. We want to "get to the bottom" of issues that have high priorities for us. Yet we have to keep reminding ourselves that the bigger the problem, the more time and care it generally takes to make real progress on it. There is nothing automatic about systems thinking. For important questions, using it effectively takes hard work and time.

There are several other examples of this pothole, some quite subtle. Ignoring the warning, for instance, that your problem statement must be put forth objectively and not imply a cause, always risks falling into this pit. The lure of doing this, of course, can be very strong, since experienced educators have a great deal of knowledge and expertise in addressing problems and often have a pretty good "inkling" about what is going on.

To have a "pet root cause" up your sleeve is to overlook the real possibility of data that shows it to be a fraudulent player in the whole enterprise. And the price one pays for this is that addressing the wrong cause of your problem will (1) gain you nothing at all, since you've hit the wrong culprit, and (2) lose you a good deal, since you will have already expended energy and resources and time to gain you nothing.

In addition, having a favorite root cause at the beginning of your process compounds the dilemma even more, since it is bound to curtail the collaborative brainstorming that is needed to seek the cause. This will surely constrain thinking about practical solutions, wind up driving the conversation into much narrower paths, and inescapably send signals to your colleagues that you don't really need their input, since you know where the real truth lies.

When the quest to cross the finish line at all costs seriously weakens the genuinely collegial atmosphere that is essential to successful leadership, the damage can be considerable. Leaders, we have persistently argued, foster as much freedom and innovation as possible among their colleagues. To push the process into a particular outcome is to push colleagues into a corner.

How to avoid this trap? First, make absolutely sure that no cause is implied in the problem statement, put there by you or anyone else. Look for some hidden implications of this smuggling, for example, in phrases such as "because of x, a situation exists that . . ." or "due to an increase/decrease in volume, a problem has occurred . . ." In addition, and although the statement might be objectively stated, you still might think in your heart of hearts that you know what the root cause actually is. Try hard, then, to keep open to the possibility that you are dead wrong about it all, and let the brainstorming process work its full weight and avoid devaluing other points of view.

"Pet" theories always make dreadful actual pets, since they can turn and bite the mind that fed them.

THE BLAME GAME

We have tried to make the strongest possible case that authentic leaders treat the partners they lead as adults whose autonomy and professionalism are valued and enhanced. There are times, however, when even the best leaders have to resist the temptation to lose sight of this lesson. These are the times when (1) high priority issues have to be addressed, (2) significant and measurable progress on them has to be made, and (3) there is a prescribed time frame within which the progress has to be demonstrated. On such occasions, the effective leader must, as we have said, *not push, not pull, but make doubly sure to lead.*

Consider the action plan of a task force with a number of objectives assigned to particular people who are charged with accomplishing specific tasks at particular times with agreed-upon indicators. It might be, for example, a project to introduce a new science curriculum by opening day of the new school year. Let's say that Bob and Sue are each responsible for objectives that, although different, require that they collaborate and cooperate, schedule things tightly, and team up to get the best use of the district's limited resources.

Well, for whatever reasons we can imagine, Bob doesn't get his task done on time. And his colleague, Sue, misses her target date as well. To explain his lack of progress, Bob accuses Sue of not sharing data that was essential to the completion of his task. Sue, of course, points the finger at Bob and claims he has been dragging his feet on analyzing the data she has given him, analysis that she needed to address the issue she was responsible for. Bob then claims the data was not relevant or worth analyzing. Sue responds that Bob wouldn't know relevant data if it had neon lights and landed on his nose.

Sound vaguely familiar? Since the name-calling has to run out of steam sometime, how long do we think it will take before both Bob and Sue start turning the Blame Game around and focus on attacking the new process they were required to follow? They got along without explicit action plans for many years, right? So who needs them? They're professionals and their judgments have always been trusted, right? And taking too much time to evaluate data isn't really necessary, since all that needs to be done is to implement the curriculum and then see how it's working.

If things go wrong, we'll address them later. Isn't that the way we've always worked?

We've noted earlier in our discussions that the people in any organization often greet changes in processes and policy with resistance as their first reaction. *This is where leaders have to play an absolutely essential role.* Reasons for the change and how we will talk about and measure progress have to be seriously and honestly communicated, and concerns about the change from those who will be affected have to be listened to and addressed. Training and time must be invested and allowance for mistakes needs to be built into the implementation.

Yet, leaders have to still insist that *professionals take full responsibility for what they have agreed to undertake,* and make it clear that passing the blame for failure onto others or onto the new process will simply *not be acceptable.* The Blame Game is an Excuse Game, and even the small residue of an excuse-riddled mindset is incompatible with the serious quest for the excellence that high achievement brings.

ORGANIZATIONAL AMNESIA

The same people in a school or school district who resist change—the Bobs and Sues of any complex enterprise—might be very different in many other ways, in spite of their agreement that they need excuses to get out of tight corners of their own making. Complex organizations not only have, but require, workers of different skills, skill levels, personal values, views of the importance of the jobs they do, beliefs about the need to work with others, and many other dissimilarities as well.

The monolithic enterprise, whether a school, a business, or a political society is not only inconceivable, but rather frightening as well, since it is not a genuinely human way of associating. It is much more suggestive of classic totalitarian nightmares. Why, then, do we sometimes expect this incredibly diverse group of professionals to be of one mind or the same feeling about the messages we send, the policies we implement, or the changes we introduce? No educator or educational leader would ever take seriously the proposition that all students are the same, learn in the same way, and have the same values, skills, or interests.

Yet managers and executives we have worked with often foolishly think that issuing a standard memo, press release, or information kit to employees is all it takes to get them to respond to the message in a similar way. And the expectation is even more bizarre when leaders are introducing a whole new way of analyzing and processing data, measuring outcomes, and working in teams. To expect that everyone in a school district will respond to being trained in systems thinking and leadership lessons in the same way and at the same rate is a formula for definitive disillusion and unsurprising wreckage.

Again, authentic leadership has to play the central role to insure that the one-size-fits-all thinking does not derail the journey to high achievement. In communicating the need for the implementation of data-based processes, those who are ultimately in charge of the district must make it clear that they not only expect their educational professionals to use the tools at different rates, but that they *actually encourage variations in the use of those tools,* since innovation and freedom are at the root of a culture of excellence.

What's more, there are diverse areas in the school system that will require differing types of execution and rates of completion by their very nature. The child study team will, obviously, have a distinct set of objectives, divergent data and specific types of measurement than, say, the science departments. Arts, language, and social studies clearly conceptualize and cash-in their data and analyses differently than physical education.

Yet, having communicated this important message, the leadership must also underscore the critical point that (1) the overall mission, vision, values, and goals of the *district are not up for individual interpretation,* for these are what focuses and unifies all of this diversity and makes the district as a whole meaningfully in pursuit of excellence, and (2) the diversity of people and departments cannot entail excuses for missing key responsibilities and dates in action plans that have been agreed upon. The image of a great symphony orchestra would be a good one to keep in mind here. Each section, each musician has a particular and special part to play so that the whole orchestral piece can be successfully played. The individual roles have to be different, but all must work together in mutual dependency so that the vision can be realized.

CONSPIRACY THEORY

When we discussed introducing change and the way people react to it earlier on, we pointed out that the right course of action is to take matters slowly and keep communicating, supporting, and encouraging those affected by the change. Educational leaders, however, sometimes tell us that they also have to be "realistic" about human nature, or at least the human nature of a few of their professional colleagues.

Some of them will simply not accept any change, no matter how much time and careful effort the leadership puts into introducing the new tools. In fact, one or two of these "bad apples" not only resist the change to process thinking, we are told, but can even take on the role of saboteurs who work constantly to undermine it to assure its failure. In so doing they might believe that they are doing the schools system a great favor.

We are not, as we have noted before, promising that Utopia will magically push its way over the doorstep once the school district focuses on the lessons of authentic leadership and the power of systems-thinking tools. And, yes, every organization, even those that win awards for excellence, has a few people in it who do not fully buy into the policies and practices that led them to being so awarded. Such nonplayers, however, are generally very few in number, if the leadership has done and continues to do its job properly. And it does not automatically follow that they are necessarily people who seek to destroy the new approach to doing business, that is, saboteurs who are leading some kind of conspiracy to cause the downfall of the new policy.

To begin to think this way, of course, can sometimes lead to a kind of paranoia, which is a condition that destroys effective leadership at its very core. If there is true reason to conclude that some professionals in the school district have not become convinced of the merit of using the new tools, *the tools themselves should be used to address the issue.* In honest discussions with colleagues who are supportive of the tools, these kinds of questions need to be answered:

- On the basis of what actual data—not rumor or supposition—do we know that there are problems with some people accepting the change?
- What might be the root cause of the lack of involvement in the process?
- What interventions would have the best practical chance of changing the situation?
- Have we done enough to explain the importance of the new approach and why it is essential that everyone support it?

Obviously, there might be truth to the belief that one or two people or three are not only not on board, but actually doing damage to the new ways of working on our crucial issues, and therefore doing harm to the mission and vision of the educational enterprise. When there are not any alternatives, of course, something more drastic will have to be done. Yet long before more severe and final moves are made, the full, data-driven picture must be analyzed and carefully evaluated. "Ready-fire-aim" is always to be guarded against.

FIRE-FIGHTING

A great poet has told us all we need to know about what can sometimes happen to even the best-laid plans of mice and men. One superintendent we have worked with suggested that the sentence could serve as the unchallenged motto of almost any school district. The dozens of small and not-so-small emergencies that crop up during any school day, not to mention a few on weekends as well, are a constant fact of any educational leader's life story.

It is not surprising, therefore, that these unplanned interruptions in the flow of a typical school week might seem to put at risk the successful implementation of a new set of practices and tools designed to move the district closer to a culture of excellence. How is it possible to give full attention and focus to making this major cultural shift, one might argue, when there is a continual need to extinguish one unexpected blaze after another?

While we appreciate the reality of this area of the educational leader's busy life, there are a few things that need to be said about it. They might not be models of solace, but they could put some helpful spin on the issue.

One principal aim of installing data-driven process thinking into a school district is to get much of the usual fire-fighting under markedly better control. The sometimes frenzied days that occur in a school district—phenomena on occasion used as one more excuse to avoid making significant changes in its normal procedure—can and will be *more effectively and efficiently handled by using the tools* we have been discussing in earlier chapters. Among the other valuable things these tools do for any organization is better and more productive use of professional time through clear and useful guidelines for priority setting and a sharper focus on what is most important to its mission, vision, values, and goals.

This might sound to some, perhaps, like a Catch 22 point to make, or at least a chicken-and-egg position. Or, as one of the educators we worked with exclaimed to us: "Look, where the heck am I going to get the time to learn about time management?"

Well, these frequent "emergency" interruptions do not happen only in school districts. Every organization of any considerable size, whether a government agency, a corporation, or major nonprofit has to face up to them at some point, or it will pay a serious price in productivity. The leaders of the high-performing organizations we discussed in an earlier chapter found ways to introduce these dynamic concepts and methods in spite of the booming, buzzing atmosphere of unplanned commotion. They did not install it the way, say, a monument is unveiled, namely, in one dramatic gesture. Nor do they count on the one knockout punch to win the bout.

They moved the new thinking and practices into place slowly, deliberately, cautiously, and not with an approach that shut down the usual activities. They did this by not announcing the change from on high, by never proclaiming or suggesting that the normal life of the enterprise had to come to a halt. They made it crystal clear that all major players had to be involved in the change. They took the time to show all players the value of simply focusing on small things such as making visible the methods they have been using to address problems, collecting relevant data to support a decision, or formulating clear objectives paired with indicators to demonstrate accomplishment.

A useful first step is to look at the kinds of "fires" that keep demanding the attention of the administration. Is every one of them a major blaze? Does every "fire" need to be put out immediately? Can some of them be handled at a different level than the superintendent-CEO? We've heard of a manager who had three bins on her desk. One was labeled, "Needs immediate action." The second was tagged, "Can wait at least a week." The last one read, "Where things go to die." While we are not recommending this simplistic three-part philosophy, there is a lot to be said for the underlying sentiment: *if everything needs immediate action, then the idea of priority-setting has become meaningless. If everything is critically important, then nothing is ever critically important.*

Most importantly, the leadership of high-performance organization, including many first-rate school districts, makes changes collaboratively and cooperatively.[1] If we agree that authentic leaders are not on power trips and are constantly into the job of making new leaders, then such leaders do not drop major new programs like a ton of bricks onto the heads of those they lead. Yet, if we are truly serious about moving our school district closer to a high-achieving enterprise, we must concentrate on getting the change made and not giving in to the claim that there is just no time to get it done.

BLURRED VISION

The vision of an organization, we know, is what it aspires to be or become. The vision is part and parcel of the strategic premise that serves as the framework against which major decisions about policies and practices have to be evaluated. The final pothole we'll briefly mention is, in a way, the summit toward which all of the previous ones lead.

Whether frustration with the process takes over, or whether we settle for good enough, or whether we play the Blame Game, and so on, by falling into these holes we are putting the aspiration toward excellence at risk. And inevitably the vision loses whatever power it had.

The mission, the values, and the goals of your school district are essential to a culture of excellence; we have been stating in unequivocal terms throughout this book. The vision is the embodiment of what that culture of excellence looks like, feels like. It is the conceptual image, therefore, of the high achievement that needs to pervade all of what we do, all of what we think and all of what we plan for.

The vision is your aspiration. It should function like a strong magnet pulling everything in one direction—mission, values, goals—and pulling all of us in our school district toward what we want and have agreed that we need to be. To the degree that any of these potholes are not handled well, that vision is diminished in its magnetic attraction, turning the journey to high achievement into a trip without a true destination.

It is no accidental fact that many of the high-performing organizations we admire make the clarity of the vision a major part not simply of their communications and training. They use it as a component in their daily operational lives, a component almost impossible to ignore. The vision statement is in evidence on almost every wall and public place in the building. It is on the business cards, the stationary, and internal notepads.

You will often see it prominently displayed on the enterprise's website and on the newsletter and press releases. Departments and divisions celebrate employee achievements by making sure there is a connection pointed out between individual and team accomplishments and how what was done can be seen as bringing the organization closer to its vision.

The lesson should be unambiguous. Blurred vision equals blurred action. It is as dangerous to high achievement as driving your car without good working headlights. Not only is it difficult to now know where you are going, but staying on the road to it has also become a pretty tricky experience.

ONE OR TWO CONCLUDING THOUGHTS

There are all kinds of potholes, obstacles, and unexpected creatures that might dart across the path as we begin moving from the comfort of our home base. The new place that we need to be, however, is essential to our becoming the best we can be, no matter what tries to stop us. We've discussed the barriers that good educational leaders in our experience have faced and have tried to handle in different ways.

New ones, no doubt, can crop up on the road in ways that we have not foreseen. And some might certainly be big enough and dangerous enough to deserve the name "sink holes" into which might fall much of the infrastructure that dedicated educational leaders and professionals have worked so hard to build. These might be severe and punitive budget cuts, political games played in a town or state at the expense of education excellence, new regulations that have all the value of news from nowhere.

The school district with authentic leadership and solid and true commitment to a systems-thinking approach to its mission, vision, values, and goals—the MVVG we keep stressing—will *always have the best chance of staying the course.* This is not just any trip, after all, but *a moral journey that matters more than anything to our children's and our society's future.* There are no guarantees, of course, and the tools we have been recommending will not automatically take root without real and far-reaching work. One always has to be realistic about the obstacles facing the journey.

Still, we have to be on guard to make sure that our "realism" doesn't slowly and imperceptibly change over into pessimism. This is why Warren Bennis in his great book *Organizing Genius* tells us that "Great Groups are optimistic, not realistic." Yes, we all want to think of ourselves as realists, as people who always need to be on watch for false ideas and flimsy schemes. Realism, however, can easily slide into negativism without awareness and without alarm bells going off. Constantly and exclusively focusing on the difficulties you face in your professional life can easily give rise to the culture of excuses. Defeating those excuses is essential if we are to get closer to the culture of excellence that high achievement in education demands.

Enough for now about the problems you might have to overcome.

You are ready to move. Your bags are already packed.

Good luck on your journey to a high-achieving school!

IDEAS FOR FURTHER CONSIDERATION

We do not for a moment believe that we have exhausted all the obstacles that might stand in the way of changing the culture of your school district by the discussion of the potholes in this chapter. Here is an exercise that might make the issue more personally and more concretely connected to your school or school district. It is directed to the superintendent or chief educational officer in a district.

Using the brainstorming methods described in chapter 4, have the leaders of key teams throughout the district conduct sessions with their teams focused on the following question:

> "What barriers stand in the way of our becoming the best school district in the United States of America within the next five years?"

You should do this with your own leadership team as well. When a list of major barriers have been agreed upon and tabulated, share the results throughout the district and ask for responses (anonymous, if the responder prefers) as to what might be done about them. The rules for the responses include no name-calling and no blame-claiming. Use the best responses to build an agenda for the periodic retreats your district holds or special meeting you convene, making sure that the recommendations of those retreats are shared throughout the entire district at every level, including board, students, and parents.

NOTE

1. Yes, we keep saying this and we are never, ever going to apologize for it!

Appendix A: The Lessons of Authentic Leadership

Lesson 1: *Discriminate Between Surface and Substance*

Develop a continuous questioning spirit
Foster that spirit throughout the organization

Lesson 2: *Confront the Likelihood of Self-Deception*

Distinguish between vision and hallucination
Settle only for facts, not mythology

Lesson 3: *Lead through Moral Character*

Solid values are essential to integrity
Without integrity you cannot have credibility

Lesson 4: *Make New Leaders, Not Disciples*

Bring out the right stuff in your people
Do not stuff your people full of right

Lesson 5: *Promote True Freedom and Innovation*

Good people have good ideas
Only good ideas have good consequences

Lesson 6: *Test Your Assumptions by the Logic of Results*

Never measure the water's depth with both feet
Live in the real world with a really open mind

Lesson 7: *Avoid Power Trips and Authority Traps*

Don't confuse your title with your leadership
All power, we know in our hearts, tends to corrupt

Lesson 8: *Do Not Simply Utter the Truth—Perform It!*

Your true native language is Action.
In the end, leaders must actually lead!

Appendix B: An Authentic Leader's Self-Assessment

We would like you to rate yourself on the Lessons of Authentic Leadership discussed earlier on in the book by using this self-assessment, an instrument we have used in our *Academy for Education Leaders*. It is not a test and you should not take it too seriously. The aim is simply to get you thinking in the right direction about your leadership practices. Not all items in the list might apply appropriately to you. For example, several are aimed at the senior leader in a school or district. Nevertheless, most will be useful for a general evaluation of the current leadership atmosphere, if not always the leader. There are a few ideas at the conclusion of the questionnaire that might help address some of your personal findings.

Using a 1-to-5 scale (where 5 = always, 4 = often, 3 = sometimes, 2 = very seldom, and 1 = never) see how you stack up on the following questions.

1. My key staff members are clear about the values and beliefs that guide my actions and decisions for the district. ___
2. I am viewed by the major stakeholders in our district as a person of credibility whose word and commitments can be trusted. ___
3. In our district one can find strong congruence between the values our professionals hold and the core values of the organization. ___
4. Our district's vision is used as the criterion against which we evaluate new practices, programs, and policies. ___
5. In our district there is in evidence an undeniable atmosphere that people feel passionate about our mission, values, and goals. ___
6. In our district, most people believe that we can be among the very best in the world at what we do. ___
7. When communicating with my key staff members, I try to underscore my sense of pride in our accomplishments and our uniqueness. ___
8. I emphasize the vision and shared values of our district when I address my staff and faculty in formal and informal settings. ___
9. I emphasize the vision and shared values of our district when I speak to my board and other stakeholders in the community. ___
10. I signal to my key staff professionals that I am genuinely interested in feedback from them on my own performance. ___

11. The professionals at all levels of our district would describe me as someone who is very interested in their personal growth. ___
12. I tend to reinforce the behavior I want shown by my key staff people. ___
13. When I make major decisions affecting our educational mission, I seek as much input from my key staff as possible. ___
14. I believe that most people who work in our district are trying to do as good a job as they can. ___
15. I openly and publicly acknowledge the contributions of others in our school or district. ___
16. People would describe me as an engaged, active listener. ___
17. When new programs and projects are tried in our district, they are looked upon as opportunities to succeed, not challenges that might fail. ___
18. Most of my professional staff would describe me as a nondogmatic leader who is open to the influence of other points of view. ___
19. I prefer face-to-face interactions with people, rather than communicating with them by memo, e-mail, or phone. ___
20. When problems arise in our district, my key staff believes that I am interested in finding the cause and not seeking someone to blame. ___
21. When I challenge or question a position or recommendation given to me, the purpose of the question is clear to my listeners. ___
22. Everyone in our district understands that we have very high expectations for performance. ___
23. Everyone in our district understands that I have set very high expectations for myself. ___
24. One of my central aims as an educational leader in our district is to encourage constant collaboration in decision making. ___
25. My key staff people have the authority to make decisions within their areas of expertise without first checking with me. ___
26. Our district publicly celebrates the achievements of our people. ___
27. The professionals in our district clearly understand that working together for a common purpose is more effective than working alone. ___
28. I view one of my highest purposes as a leader to be a major change agent for our school or our district. ___
29. The cultural environment of our district would be characterized by outsiders as one that promotes the open and nonthreatening exchange of ideas. ___
30. Project teams in our district are imbued with a clear sense of the imperative need to connect their recommendations to the mission, vision, values, and goals we have established for the district. ___

31. I believe my position as a leader requires me to seek the moral high ground in dealing with all stakeholders in the district. ___
32. I believe that others would characterize my leadership style as strong-minded but also a style that aims to enlist others. ___
33. Over and above our educational mission, communicating with and adding value to our community is one of my essential aims as a leader. ___
34. I encourage all the professionals in our district to constantly question the status quo in order to look for improvements. ___
35. I think of the professionals in our district more as colleagues than as followers. ___

SOME NEXT STEPS

For each item on which you are a "3" or less you might want to ask a few questions. The answers to them will require no quick fix but some serious reflection.

For example, suppose you rated yourself a "3" on number 18, that is, you think most of your professional staff would only *sometimes* describe you as nondogmatic and open to other points of view.

(a) What is it about your interaction with them at times that might lead them to describe you this way? What signals are you sending them—either through the words you are using or the body language and tone of voice—that suggest you really don't normally want to hear opposing views? Are there any particular examples that stand out in recent past interactions that you think might have been particularly emblematic to staff of your not being open to the input of others?

(b) How can you get better at this? What is it going to take to really improve?

You can begin by being clearly conscious of your behavior when meeting or conversing with your staff, and you should try to develop a routine for the kinds of questions and comments you would make during these encounters. Your aim is to show genuine interest in other points of view, show that you are taking them seriously, and look for the value in them. Look also at your written communications to the staff; do they show an authoritative tone rather than sense of genuine personal connection?

(c) How will you *know* you are getting better at this?

The answer is simple in this case—don't be afraid to share the idea. You should tell your staff that you, in fact, genuinely value their opinions but are not sure that your intention to express it always comes across to them. Tell them that you are trying to be sure they know this and that you are working on it consciously. You will have set a great example for them about honesty and credibility as well. If you're getting it right, the newer atmosphere in your meetings and conversations will soon be evident.

Another idea: you might also have given a low rating not directly to yourself but indirectly, that is, on the way the district is functioning. For instance, suppose you rated item number 6 a "3" or lower, namely, that the district doesn't appear to have a passion for excellence. What can you do to inspire the majority of your professionals to really believe, to truly buy into the vision, to be more passionate about the quest to be the best in the world (or "on a mission from God" to quote Warren Bennis)? Is it a question of inspiration, or is there something else at work? Are there any organizational issues that are acting as barriers? Have you talked to your key staff to get some ideas about these barriers and how they might be addressed?

Again, these questions and others like them need to be honestly asked. And they put us back into *IDEAS*, for these key questions boil down to what *causes* might be responsible for the situation, what possible *solutions* should be carefully considered to address the causes, and what are the best ways to *deploy* them?

Some final thoughts: it's advisable to concentrate on one or two items to begin with, not to try to do all of them at once. That approach will make for certain failure. Developing and improving your leadership skill is not an over-and-done operation or a one-trick pony. It is a constant journey that even the best leaders of the best organizations have to constantly travel, and the only way to travel it is one step at a time. Leadership, we've said, is about building and keeping strong connections with others, and the most valuable connections are the durable ones between people, not superiors and inferiors.

All relationships, however, are persistently and frequently changing. The key to the journey is honest reflection on *where you can improve, why you should improve, and how you can improve.* Your leadership has already been consistently demonstrated by your own successful careers in education. Authentic leadership, however, is a challenge that requires constant commitment to get better. You have made a huge and important start by carefully and seriously working through these pages and the issues they have been addressing.

You are already on your way. Good luck for great and sustained leadership!

Appendix C: *IDEAS* Project Report Template

Project Title:_____
Project Champion:_____ Date Initiated:_____
Target End Date:_____

Identify the Problem
    Problem Statement Criteria:

- The statement is specific, objective, and describes a measurable outcome
- The statement relates the effect in a way that can be measured
- The statement is objective: no causes are mentioned nor a solution is implied
- The statement focuses on the gap between what is and what should be
- The statement reflects the pain caused by the gap

Determine the Root Cause
    Root Cause Analysis Questions:

- What are possible root causes?
- Which causes have the greatest impact?
- What data is needed to support assumptions about root causes?
- What data is needed to measure the impact of the causes?
- What are the sources of the data (e.g., people, performance results)?
- Which causes have the greatest impact based on the data collected?

Explore Possible Solutions
    Possible solution(s) and questions to ask:

- What possible solutions could eliminate the root cause(s)?
- Which solutions will have the greatest impact on eliminating the root cause?
- Which solutions are the most cost-effective?
- Which solutions can be feasibly implemented?

Assess the Results
    Action Plan Criteria/Questions:

- What actions will be required to implement the solution?

- Is the champion or leader of each action clearly stated?
- What resources will be required for action items?
- What are the timelines/milestones or expected completion dates?
- How will we measure the success of the plan?

Standardize the Improvement
Identifying the next step(s) and questions to ask:

- Whose approval is needed to implement the action plan?
- What preliminary steps must be taken to gain the necessary support that will ensure a successful outcome?
- What are the questions that have not been answered?

Appendix D: Additional Resources

There are hundreds—perhaps thousands—of books on educational leadership and high-performing organizations. There are dozens more of the good ones that could have been added to this list. We offer these as the writings that have particularly influenced us and that we believe are particularly relevant to the tools we have been discussing. If there are others that have been important to your own professional growth as educational leaders, we hope you will take the time to share them with us. You can contact us through our publisher Rowman & Littlefield Education Division.

Abbate, Fred J. "Education Leadership in a Culture of Compliance," *Phi Delta Kappan* 91, no. 6 (March 2010): 35–37.
Baldrige Performance Excellence Program. *2011 – 2012 Education Criteria for Performance Excellence*. Washington, DC: National Institute of Standards and Technology.
Bennis, Warren. *On Becoming a Leader*. Philadelphia: Perseus Publishing, 2009.
Bennis, Warren, and Patricia Ward Biederman. *Organizing Genius: The Secrets of Creative Collaboration*. Boston: Addison-Wesley, 1997.
Blanchard, Ken, et al. *Leading at a Higher Level*. Upper Saddle River, NJ: FT Press, 2010.
Brache, Alan P. *How Organizations Work: Taking a Holistic Approach to Enterprise Health*. San Francisco: Wiley, 2002.
Burns, James MacGregor. *Leadership*. New York: Harper & Row, 1978.
Byham, William C. *Zapp in Education*. New York: Ballantine Books, 1992.
Collins, Jim. *Good to Great and the Social Sectors*. Boulder, CO: Jim Collins, 2005.
Freedman, Mike, with Benjamin B. Tregoe. *The Art and Discipline of Strategic Leadership*. McGraw-Hill, 2003.
Fullan, Michael, ed. *Educational Leadership*. San Francisco: Jossey-Bass, 2000.
———. *Leading in a Culture of Change*. San Francisco: Jossey-Bass, 2001.
Kotter, John P. *Leading Change*. New York: Free Press, 1996.
———. *Corporate Culture and Performance*. New York: Free Press, 2011.
Kouzes, James M., and Barry Z. Posner. *The Leadership Challenge*. San Francisco: Wiley, 2012.
Orsini, Joyce, and Diana Deming Cahill, eds. *The Essential Deming: Leadership Principles from the Father of Quality*. New York: McGraw-Hill, 2012.
Pfeffer, Jeffery. *What Were They Thinking? Unconventional Wisdom about Management*. Boston: Harvard Business School Press, 2007.
Quinn, Robert E. *Deep Change: Discovering the Leader Within*. San Francisco: Jossey-Bass, 1996.
Sahlberg, Pasi. *Finnish Lessons: What Can the World Learn from Educational Change in Finland?* New York: Teachers College Press, 2011.
Senge, Peter M. *The Fifth Discipline: The Art and Practice of the Learning Organization*. New York: Doubleday, 2006.
Storr, Anthony. *Feet of Clay: Saints, Sinners, and Madmen: A Study of Gurus*. New York: Free Press, 1997.
Walton, Mary. *The Deming Management Method*. New York: Perigee Books, 1988.

Weiss, Alan. *Managing for Peak Performance: A Guide to the Power (and Pitfalls) of Personal Style*. New York: Harper & Row, 1989.
Wren, J. Thomas, ed. *The Leader's Companion: Insights on Leadership through the Ages*. New York: Free Press, 1995.
Zenger, John H., and Joseph Folkman. *The Extraordinary Leader: Turning Good Managers into Great Leaders*. New York: McGraw-Hill, 2002.

Glossary

Action Plan an outline containing the details of who will do what action by when

Affinitizing the process of grouping ideas together based on their similarity

Bar Chart data that is displayed graphically, showing frequency either over time or by individual categories

Beliefs tenets we hold to be true, even if evidence for them is less than absolutely conclusive

BHAG acronym that stands for: big hairy audacious goal, used by Jim Collins in *Good to Great*

Brainstorming the process of soliciting many ideas to focus on quantity versus quality

Consensus decision making that implies all aspects have been explored and all can support the decision of the group

Continuous improvement the philosophical outlook of never being satisfied with the current performance level

Critical Few the most significant items that remain in an evaluated list of ideas such as causes, solutions, or actions

Customer-Driven the concept of structuring processes and methods based on customer requirements, not the needs of the organization

Flowchart a graphic depiction of the sequence of events in producing an outcome

Goals what is to be achieved in the longer term

Hedgehog from *Good to Great* by Jim Collins—the intersection of what we can be best in the world at, what we are passionate about, and what drives our resource engine

IDEAS standardizing the improvement problem-solving process; acronym for: identifying the problem; determining the root cause; exploring possible solutions; and assessing the results

Involvement by Everyone concept of engaging all stakeholders in the process of accomplishing a goal or task

JTHAS whole school reform model; the acronym that stands for: *The Journey to High-Achieving Schools*

Leaders those individuals that know the way, go the way and show the way

Leadership the practice of taking others to a performance level that they may not have otherwise taken

Mission the unique purpose or reason why an organization or team exists

Multivoting a technique for reducing a large list of items down to a manageable few items by limiting the number of votes that can be cast

MVVG acronym standing for Mission, Vision, Values, and Goals

Nominal Group Technique a method by which items are evaluated against each other in order to reach a consensus in a group

PDCA continuous improvement model; acronym stands for: Plan-Do-Check-Act

PDSA version of the PDCA model adopted by schools; the acronym stands for: Plan-Do-Study-Act

Prioritizing technique of applying a weighted vote to a list of items; for example, using a numerical range such as 9-3-1

Problem Statement an objective description of the issue at hand or current situation

Process-Centered concept of defining and measuring activities to ensure the desired outcome is consistently delivered

Quality the characteristic of meeting or exceeding relevant and essential expectations such as customer or client needs

SIPOC a tool that results in a graphic depiction of a system; acronym stands for: Suppliers Input Processes Outputs Customer

SMOGP acronym that defines problem statement structure; stands for: Specific, Measurable, Objectively-stated (indicating a) Gap and the Pain involved by not addressing the problem

Systems Perspective viewpoint that uses the methods of systems thinking with an emphasis on process, data, and measurement of results

Values enduring beliefs through which our decisions are made

Vision our view of what we aspire to be or become

Why Five Times root cause analysis technique to get to the most basic cause

About the Authors

Fred J. Abbate is the former president and chief executive officer of the New Jersey Utilities Association (NJUA), a position he held from 1995 to July 2006. Fred holds a PhD from Columbia University, a master's degree from Boston College, and an AB from Fairfield University. Prior to joining NJUA, he held numerous executive and managerial positions for Atlantic Energy. As a loaned executive from the company, he served for a year as director of Leadership New Jersey, the state's best known public policy leadership program. He is currently a senior associate with the Performance Excellence Group. Fred has managed major consulting projects involving leadership, strategic planning, human resource development, and communications for numerous business and trade associations, government agencies, colleges, and corporations.

He is the author of two books on political theory and contemporary philosophy, and has published numerous articles on decision making, politics, leadership, legal theory, educational reform, and strategic planning and has chaired and worked with leading key communications, customer research, and industry policy committees for the Edison Electric and the Electric Power Research Institutes. Fred was also certified as a Kepner-Tregoe trainer and a Blessing/White program leader. Before joining Atlantic Energy, he taught at Rutgers University, Iona College, and the New York City University. He is presently on the faculty of the Pennoni Honors College of Drexel University and in 2010 he was given the inaugural Award by the College for Outstanding Teaching.

Ken Biddle is the founder and president/CEO of the Performance Excellence Group, LLC (PEG). He is also the former executive director of Quality New Jersey, which was the administrator of the New Jersey Governor's Award for Performance Excellence. Prior to forming PEG, he managed one-fifth of the revenue and profitability of Six-Sigma Qualtec, Inc., a global organization providing services to Fortune 500 companies. His experience spans over twenty-five years, developing implementation strategies for all aspects of management improvement, along with assisting in the successful execution of those strategies. Prior to becoming a consultant, he was a quality director at the Defense Supply Center in Philadelphia where he fostered change by developing and implementing process-centered improvement strategies. The improvement strategies significantly contributed to the center being awarded the federal government agencies' equivalent of the Malcolm Baldrige National Quality Award.

While attending several University of Tennessee Institutes for Productivity through Quality, Ken was introduced to highly sophisticated data-driven improvement methods. This, combined with his extensive experience as a Baldrige examiner, served as the catalyst for his appreciation of systems thinking as a means of achieving performance excellence. He currently uses systems thinking in deploying various organizational development, improvement, and change management techniques, which includes strategic planning, problem solving, and six sigma. Through PEG, Ken is instilling these research-based leadership and improvement methods into K–12 schools, in addition to nonprofit organizations and businesses alike.

Joseph M. Tomaselli has been an educator for more than thirty years, including having served as a teacher, guidance counselor, project director, principal, board of education member, adjunct professor, and an executive administrator for a statewide quality education initiative.

Joe created the Achievement-Based Character Development Program, which was the foundation for improving academic achievement; creating and sustaining a safe school climate; raising the satisfaction of the staff, students, and all other stakeholders; and creating partnerships with local business, government, and community groups. Joe coauthored "Character Development in Education: The ABCDs of Valuing," which was published in the April 1996 issue of the NASSP Bulletin and explains the program.

www.ingramcontent.com/pod-product-compliance
Lightning Source LLC
Chambersburg PA
CBHW051814230426
43672CB00012B/2733